D1377836

Managing Workplace Bullying

MANAGING WORKPLACE BULLYING

HOW TO IDENTIFY, RESPOND TO AND MANAGE BULLYING BEHAVIOR IN THE WORKPLACE

Aryanne Oade
Director, Oade Associates Limited

First published 2009 by
PALGRAVE MACMILLAN

Palgrave Macmillan in the UK is an imprint of Macmillan Publishers Limited, registered in England, company number 785998, of Houndmills, Basingstoke, Hampshire RG21 6XS.

Palgrave Macmillan in the US is a division of St Martin's Press LLC, 175 Fifth Avenue, New York, NY 10010.

Palgrave Macmillan is the global academic imprint of the above companies and has companies and representatives throughout the world.

Palgrave® and Macmillan® are registered trademarks in the United States, the United Kingdom, Europe and other countries

ISBN-13: 978-0-230-22808-5

This book is printed on paper suitable for recycling and made from fully managed and sustained forest sources. Logging, pulping and manufacturing processes are expected to conform to the environmental regulations of the country of origin.

A catalogue record for this book is available from the British Library.

A catalog record for this book is available from the Library of Congress.

10 9 8 7 6 5 4 3 2 1
18 17 16 15 14 13 12 11 10 09

Printed and bound in CPI Antony Rowe, Chippenham and Eastbourne.

About the Author

Aryanne Oade is a Chartered Psychologist, coach, workshop facilitator and author. She is the owner of a successful and established coaching and development practice which mixes business psychology with the skills of professional actors. Aryanne set up her business in 1994. Since then she has designed and delivered over 130 bespoke executive coaching programs and over 100 tailored professional skills workshops for leaders, managers and employees of client organizations across the UK, Europe and North America. Some of these projects have involved working with clients on the reality of handling bullying behavior at work. Aryanne has coached people being bullied, those employing bullying behavior, team colleagues of peoplebeing bullied and the managers of bullies.

Note from the Author

This book focuses on how to identify and manage bullying behavior at work. In writing the book I am offering you, the reader, my experiences and know-how as someone who has coached and worked with clients on many issues involving workplace bullying. I am not seeking to advise you on how to handle your specific workplace relationships, but rather to offer you my insights as someone who has coached and worked with many clients on these challenging issues.

Every situation is unique so, in addition to reading this book, those of you who are subject to workplace bullying might want to consult your HR department or refer to your employer's anti-bullying policy, should these resources be available to you. You might also want to seek the services of a professional advisor skilled at helping people with the psychological, emotional and physical effects of workplace bullying: a therapist, business psychologist or health professional who should be able to offer you tailored, detailed and impartial counsel on the particular interpersonal and intrapersonal issues you might be facing as a result of your workplace experiences.

Acknowledgments

I would like to acknowledge a number of people who have played a part in my work and the writing of this book.

Firstly, my thanks and gratitude go to all the clients who have spoken with me over the years about their experiences of handling bullying behavior at work. These are among some of the most rewarding coaching conversations I have had and I appreciate that, from a client's point of view, perhaps some of the hardest to be involved in.

Next, I would like to thank the very many clients, contacts and friends with firsthand experiences of workplace bullying who allowed me to pick their brains at the start of the writing process. These conversations gave me valuable material for the examples in the book and helped me decide how to structure and focus its chapters. I send my thanks to each one of you gratefully and anonymously.

Finally, I'd also like to send my special appreciation to Julie Perry for her helpful and thoughtful critique of each of the chapters as I wrote them and to Stephen Rutt and the entire team at Palgrave Macmillan for being such effective and enjoyable coworkers.

Overview

WHO THIS BOOK IS FOR

This book is about bullying behavior at work: what it is; how to handle it effectively; how to respond if you find yourself subject to it; what to do if you work with, for or alongside a bully; what to do if you manage someone who uses bullying behavior in the workplace; and what to do to effectively support someone you know who is being bullied at work.

I wrote this book for the increasing numbers of people at work – across all four continents – who are experiencing bullying behavior at work. Specifically I wrote it for those of you who:

- Think that you might currently be subject to bullying at work – or worry that you could be in the near future.
- Have already been bullied at work and want to learn from the experience.
- Witness bullying behavior in your workplace and would like to know what to do to make sure that, should the bully turn their attention onto you, you will know how to respond constructively.
- Find yourself managing someone who uses bullying behavior.
- Are the friends or family of people being bullied, want to understand more about what your loved one is experiencing from the inside out, and want to know how to effectively support them during and after they are subject to bullying at work.

WHY I WROTE THIS BOOK

My aim in writing the book is four fold.

- Firstly: for those of you who have firsthand experience of the debilitating effects of workplace bullying, my wish is to equip you with effective tools, strategies, insight and knowledge which will give you the confidence to handle bullying behavior as and when it happens.
- Secondly: for those of you who have organizational seniority over a bully, my aim is to provide you with some effective management strategies so that you can confront the bully in a way that does convince them to alter their behavior and stop bullying – or convinces them to seek help to stop bullying.

- Thirdly: for those of you witnessing bullying behavior at work, and/or those of you who are close to someone who is being bullied, my aim is to furnish you with enough knowledge about what your friend or loved one is going through that you find ways of supporting them which they experience as supportive, understanding and helpful.
- Fourthly: for those of you who observe bullying behavior in your workplace and are discomforted by what you witness, I'd like to provide you with the wisdom, skills and tactics which will enable you to prevent yourself from becoming the next target of a bully, should they turn their attentions toward you.

WHAT THIS BOOK WILL DO FOR YOU

This book will help you to:

- Recognize what constitutes bullying behavior at work.
- Appreciate the full psychological and emotional impact of bullying behavior on the person being bullied.
- Highlight what factors cause people to use bullying behavior at work.
- Identify and select effective interpersonal strategies for handling bullying behavior in the moment it occurs.
- Understand why these tactics and strategies are effective at handling bullying behavior and interrupting the intimidating dynamic that the bully wants to perpetuate.
- Recognize how to handle the situation if you suspect that someone you manage is using bullying behavior.
- Appreciate what steps senior organizational figures need to take to influence those using bullying behavior to stop employing it.
- Understand how best to support a friend or family member who is being bullied during and after their experience of workplace bullying.

This book is full of examples of workplace bullying, each of which is set in a workplace such as a school, a bank, a hospital or a technology department. In most cases I have avoided locating these workplaces in any specific country, preferring instead to focus the action on the dynamics that are set in play when one colleague starts to use bullying behavior with another. My hope is that the book will become an effective toolkit for people across the globe as they seek to identify, respond to and manage bullying behavior at work.

MY BACKGROUND AND WORK

I am a Chartered Psychologist and have been working as a business psychologist since the late 1980s. During the following five years I worked for three consultancy firms before deciding to work as an independent business psychologist in early 1994. Some of my initial projects were carried out as an associate to smaller consultancy firms. Then, in January 2000, I set up Oade Associates to design and deliver bespoke executive coaching programs, tailored professional skills workshops and custom made conference scenarios. In this work I combine business psychology with the skills of professional actors to create real-life scenarios that reflect the people-handling, leadership, management and influencing issues that my clients deal with in their work.

In my coaching programs and workshops I ask clients to step back from their day-to-day work and workplace experiences. I ask them to reflect on the quality of the behavior they use when things are going well for them, and to compare that to what they do when they are under pressure. Then, with the help of my professional actor colleagues, I re-create the very meetings clients find most challenging – meetings which they mishandle, meetings in which they lose influence, credibility or personal power, and meetings in which they are subject to pressurizing or unreasonable tactics – and help clients to revisit these meetings using different and more productive behavior, skills and interpersonal strategies.

I coach them to understand the links between their intrapersonal world – their values, character and personality – and their interpersonal behavior: the tactics, skills and strategies they use with other people. Clients practise their new approaches until they are satisfied that they can go back to work and use them straight away, and so retain influence, control and personal power in situations which they might otherwise handle ineffectively, or, in some situations, might experience as abusive. As a result of working in this way, clients perform better in their roles, have greater influence in their key workplace relationships and demonstrate sustained behavior change.

In addition to working one-to-one and with small groups I also work with conference audiences. In this case I develop a series of custom-made sketches which my actor colleagues subsequently enact live on stage. Audience members discuss and debate the action at round tables, so that they can learn from one another's experiences of handling similar instances, and decide which interpersonal skills and tactics work well in particular situations and which don't.

The scenarios can concentrate on any workplace issue, and recent sketches have focused on responding to and handling bullying and harassing behavior at work.

HELPING CLIENTS HANDLE WORKPLACE BULLYING

Since starting to work in this way I have run hundreds of executive coaching programs, professional skills workshops and custom-made conference scenarios for clients across the UK, Europe and North America. Many of these projects involved working with clients on the reality of handling challenging, forceful or pressurizing behavior in their colleagues, customers and workplace contacts. Some of the behaviors that clients have brought to these meetings are behaviors that are best characterized as workplace bullying:

- I have worked with clients who were being bullied at the time of their coaching program. These projects focused on equipping clients with the know-how to handle the complex interpersonal and intra-personal dynamics that their experiences created for them.
- I have worked with clients who hired team members who subsequently used bullying behavior, and to whom the responsibility of confronting that unexpected behavior fell. These projects focused on equipping these clients with the interpersonal agility and resolve to confront the bully over their behavior and continue to do so until they prevailed.
- I have worked with clients who observe bullying behavior being used at work on a daily basis and who, while not subject yet to its full force themselves, feared that the bully might one day turn their attention on them. These projects focused on providing clients with the development they need to preempt this unhappy situation from arising in future and on how to handle it should it do so.

In addition to working with clients who have experienced bullying themselves I have also worked with a few clients who, however they deceived themselves about it, habitually used bullying behavior with at least one of their team members, and whose preference before working with me was to blind themselves – or to simply disregard – the consequences of their behavior for the person they systematically bullied and, indeed, for their own reputations. These projects focused on equipping the clients involved with, variously, insight into the destructive consequences of their behavior for their colleagues *and* the consequent under-performance they created in a team they were responsible for; measurement of the quality of their management and leadership of their team and development in areas of weakness; and improving their self-awareness and self-knowledge so that they could *choose* to behave differently. All of these projects except one were successful in helping the client using bully behavior to replace those tactics with effective, nonbullying management and leadership practice.

I have seen firsthand the enormous psychological, emotional and physical toll that workplace bullying can have on the people affected by it directly and indirectly. I have seen just how difficult it can be for someone without any prior training to select and employ productive, effective behavioral strategies and tactics which will preserve their self-esteem and psychological well-being while being subject to workplace bullying. I have seen how otherwise effective managers and leaders can fail to take the right actions at the right time to prevent or confront bullying activity and so, however unwittingly, enable workplace bullying. I have seen how cunning and self-deceptive bullies can be about the quality, nature and motivation behind their conduct and how their self-deceptions and justifications help them avoid the need to take responsibility for their behavior and change it.

WRITING THIS BOOK

This book comes out of my work in helping clients to develop the intrapersonal awareness and interpersonal skills they need to confront bullying behavior; maintain their boundaries when under pressure from bullying behavior; remain assertive while dealing with this form of assault; and appropriately protect their self-esteem while working with people who would otherwise injure it through the use of bullying behavior.

The Structure of the Book

OVERALL FOCUS OF THE BOOK

This book is a practical, comprehensive and personal guide suitable for people at work around the world. It will take you through a structured process that will enable you to step back from your workplace and assess the bullying behavior you encounter objectively. It will introduce you to a series of effective steps that you can take which will help you to handle the bullying dynamic more effectively. It will enable you to make sound decisions about what to do differently and better to preserve your personal power and protect yourself should you be subject to bullying behavior or fear that you might be in the future. It will also provide you with sound, effective strategies for managing a workplace bully who happens to be a member of your team, and for helping you effectively support a friend or family member who is subject to workplace bullying.

THE FIRST SEVEN CHAPTERS

Each of the first seven chapters is on one key aspect of workplace bullying. These opening chapters describe what constitutes workplace bullying, examining the nature of the bullying dynamic between a workplace bully and the person they subject to their bullying behavior. They describe what factors cause some people to start using bullying behavior at work and then outline a series of effective strategies, actions and behavior you could use to protect yourself from bullying behavior should you find yourself subject to the attentions of a workplace bully. In addition, these chapters highlight some of the challenges facing managers who realize that they have a bully in their team, and examine how to support a friend or family member who is being bullied.

These first seven chapters include a number of examples and Character Cameos that describe a series of effective tactics, skills and interpersonal strategies for handling bullying behavior at work and its effects on those subject to it.

THE EXAMPLES

Each of the examples in the book is either based on realistic workplace bullying dynamics or on a real-life instance of bullying behavior at work. In each case I have substantially changed the details of the action and characters to protect the identities of the real people involved. Following each example you will find two sections. Firstly, you'll find a section entitled 'Analysing the Dynamics' in which we will take a deeper look at the scenario depicted in the example and get behind the actions, words and behaviors of the protagonists to understand their motivations and intentions, and the best ways to handle the bullying behaviors described in the example. Following this section you'll find 'Conclusions' in which we'll draw key lessons from the example.

THE CHARACTER CAMEOS

Periodically throughout the book you will find a section entitled 'Character Cameo'. The Character Cameos help you learn more about what is motivating a particular character in an example or in the major case study which occurs toward the end of the book. Usually these characters are either people who use bullying behavior at work or are people subject to bullying behavior at work. Some of the Character Cameos are also based on real-life instances of workplace bullying and, in these cases, I have taken care to change all the details surrounding each cameo to protect the identities of the people involved.

The Character Cameos describe the conduct and actions of workplace bullies and, sometimes, the people they bully. They invite you to look behind the behaviors used by the key characters in an example and draw links between their actions and words – their interpersonal behavior – and their intrapersonal world: their personality, character and values.

THE CASE STUDY

The eighth chapter of the book takes the form of a realistic case study depicting workplace bullying. It is set in a fictional company that operates worldwide and it is designed to give you can opportunity to apply the principles presented in the first seven chapters of the book to a lifelike scenario. The scenario follows the fortunes of an employee of the company who is subject to workplace bullying, and describes how one of the senior figures in the organization reacts to the knowledge that one of his managers is consistently using bullying behavior at work. As you read the case study you will be asked to analyze it from the point of view of the employee to determine what she could do differently and better to handle the situation she finds herself in.

Following each portion of the case study you will find a section entitled 'Questions for You to Answer' and a space below each question so that you can jot down your responses to it. You will also find suggested answers to these questions at the end of the case study against which you can compare and contrast your own ideas. These answers will provide you with tips, tactics, skills and strategies which could be used to respond to the instances of bullying behavior described in the case study.

FINAL TWO CHAPTERS

The penultimate chapter in the book describes some of the common physical, emotional and psychological reactions reported by people who are subject to workplace bullying. This chapter is a resource both for those of you who are subject to an experience of workplace bullying and for those of you who are the friends or family members of someone who is being bullied at work. The last chapter in the book offers some closing thoughts on workplace bullying.

RATIONALE FOR THIS STRUCTURE

I have written the book in this way to make it as immediate and practical as possible, describing the issues surrounding workplace bullying from the point of view of people subject to it. Those of you with firsthand experience of workplace bullying will recognize the dynamics portrayed in the case study, Character Cameos and Examples. Those of you without firsthand experience of workplace bullying on which to draw, will learn what to look for and will be forearmed with effective strategies for responding to a workplace bully should you encounter one. Those of you with responsibility for managing bullying behavior in your workplace will be aware of what behaviors constitute bullying at work, what impact these behaviors have on your employees and how to effectively confront those who use them.

My hope is that, whatever your reasons for reading this book, you gain insight into why bullies use the behavior they employ and that, by the end of the book, you will have an effective toolkit of tactics, strategies and skills to use should you need to identify, respond to or manage bullying behavior at work.

The Scope of This Book

WHAT THE BOOK IS ABOUT AND WHAT YOU WON'T FIND IN IT

This book deals with bullying behavior at work. It highlights how to identify, handle and manage workplace bullying behavior and is aimed at people at work around the world and their friends and families. It focuses around the human dynamics involved in workplace bullying and identifies:

- The individual behaviors and patterns of behavior that bullies use in the workplace.
- The effect of these behaviors on the people subject to them – and on the people who witness them being used.
- The issues facing managers who need to confront a team member who is using bullying behavior.
- The pitfalls of mishandling bullying behavior and thereby failing to protect yourself from it.
- Productive ways of handling and managing bullying behavior at the time it is happening.

The book does not, however, focus on the many potentially valuable sources of help that your employing organization might be able to offer you, should you be subject to workplace bullying – or fear that you might be in the future.

These issues are beyond the scope of this book. Increasing numbers of employers make available to their employees a range of resources which can help them understand what they are going through, find practical ways of handling their experience of bullying and gain valuable organizational support as they navigate their way through it. These resources vary widely in range and quality but, at their best, can be excellent sources of advice about how to handle the situation you find yourself in and take action against the person bullying you. They include:

- Employee Assistance Programs.
- Occupational Health Departments.

- Employee Counseling Services specializing in counseling people subject to workplace bullying.
- Human Resource Departments trained in workplace bullying, its effects on people at work and the legal implications of a proven case of workplace bullying.
- Anti-Bullying and Anti-Harassment Policies which define what behavior does and does not constitute workplace bullying for a particular employer.
- Formal Anti-Bullying and Anti-Harassment Procedures which are designed to investigate alleged incidents of workplace bullying and, if proven, could lead to disciplinary action being taken against the bully.

Contents

1 **What is Workplace Bullying?: The Behaviors and Dynamics**   1
that Constitute Workplace Bullying: Your experiences of
workplace bullying; workplace bullying: a definition; the
intentions of workplace bullies; behaviors frequently used
by bullies; Example one: an incident of workplace bullying?;
an incident of workplace bullying?: analyzing the dynamics,
an incident of workplace bullying?: conclusions; Example two:
bullying in the workplace; bullying in the workplace: analyzing
the dynamics; bullying in the workplace: conclusions; your
goal in responding to workplace bullying; summary and next
chapter.

2 **Why People Bully Their Colleagues: The Psychological**   16
Profile of a Workplace Bully: The disposition of a workplace
bully; Character Cameo one: the threatened senior manager;
Character Cameo one: the intrapersonal world of the
consultant; Character Cameo two: switch of roles; Character
Cameo two: scapegoating others; Character Cameo three:
clash of styles; Character Cameo three: driven to aggressive
management; Key causes of workplace bullying; euphemisms
and excuses for bullying behavior; summary and next
chapter.

3 **Sowing The Seeds for Bullying: The First Interactions**   35
Between a Bully and Their Target: Who gets bullied at work?
three different situations in which bullies encounter potential
targets, Examples one and two: setting up bullying during
a job interview; Example one: joining the firm; joining the firm:
analyzing the dynamics; joining the firm: conclusions; Example
two: collusive bullying; collusive bullying: analyzing the
dynamics; collusive bullying: conclusions; summary and next
chapter

4 **The Bullying Dynamic: Issues of Power and Choice at**   51
The Heart of a Bullying Relationship: Creating a bullying
dynamic; working with nonbullying colleagues; working with
bullying colleagues; disregarding your boundaries and your
choices; Example one: blindsided; blindsided: analyzing the

Contents

dynamics; blindsided: conclusions; bullying bosses;
Example two: unilateral decision; unilateral decision: analyzing
the dynamics; Example three: reputational risk; reputational risk:
analyzing the dynamics; Example four: turning the tables; turning
the tables: analyzing the dynamics; the bullying
dynamic: conclusions; identifying your choices; summary and next
chapter.

5 **Resisting a Workplace Bully: Choosing to Assert Yourself,**   70
Managing Your Boundaries: Managing your boundaries:
protecting yourself; Example one: starting to bully; starting to
bully: analyzing the dynamics; starting to bully: conclusions;
starting to bully: key lessons; calling on your personal
power; Example two: commanding attention; commanding
attention: analyzing the dynamics; Example three: snide
comments; snide comments: analyzing the dynamics; feeling
powerless; reframing workplace bullying as a series of abusive
interactions; choosing not to resist; Example four: losing
power; losing power: analyzing the dynamics; losing power:
conclusions; summary and next chapter.

6 **Managing a Workplace Bully: Confronting Bullying**   92
Behavior in a Team Member: Your challenge as a manager
of a bully; Example one: bad hire; bad hire: Analyzing the
dynamics; bad hire: conclusions; Character Cameo one: the
project manager; Character Cameo two: the sales director;
Example two: confrontation; confrontation: analyzing the
dynamics; confrontation: conclusions; confronting a
workplace bully; why will this approach succeed?; Example
three: unmasked; unmasked: conclusions; confronting
a workplace bully: key lessons; Summary and next
chapter.

7 **The Role of Friends and Family Members: Supporting**   113
Someone You Know Through an Experience of Workplace
Bullying: A change in behavior; the challenge of workplace
bullying; reactions to workplace bullying; thinking different
thoughts; using adapted behavior; providing effective support;
seeking professional help; practical things you can do to help;
summary and next chapter.

8 **A Cautionary Tale: A Case Study:** Returning to work; the   127
new role; questions for you to answer: set one; Character
Cameo one: the marketing manager; a positive impression;
sloppy timekeeping?; questions for you to answer: set two;

intense job; Character Cameo two: the sales director; turn for the worse; questions for you to answer: set three; impromptu appraisal; questions for you to answer: set four; business trip; the start of the week; unexpected attack; questions for you to answer: set five; review section: answers to the questions: sets one to five; summary and next chapter.

9 **The Human Consequences of Bullying at Work: Common Emotional, Psychological and Physical Reactions to Workplace Bullying:** Different people, different reactions: common emotional and psychological reactions to workplace bullying; common physical reactions to workplace bullying; seeking professional help; helping yourself through it; summary and next chapter.   149

10 **Aftermath: Final Thoughts on Workplace Bullying:** Life after being bullied at work; putting it into perspective; your experiences of workplace bullying.   157

References, Websites and Further Reading   163

Index   165

CHAPTER 1

What is Workplace Bullying?
The Behaviors and Dynamics that Constitute Workplace Bullying

Let's begin this book with an examination of the behaviors, attitudes and dynamics which constitute workplace bullying. The chapter will start by examining your experiences of bullying in the workplace. It will then define what 'workplace bullying' is and highlight the intentions of people who use bullying behavior at work. It will move on to identify a range of behaviors that bullies often employ when bullying their colleagues before providing you with some examples to illustrate these themes. Let's start with you and your experiences of observing or handling bullying behavior at work.

YOUR EXPERIENCES OF WORKPLACE BULLYING

Workplace bullying is increasing. It is a fact that more and more people witness, observe or are subject to behavior which is characterized by bullying while they go about their normal workplace duties. Most people go to work expecting to be able to carry out their workplace assignments in an atmosphere which is conducive to effective performance and which is psychologically and emotionally safe. Sadly, as the incidents of workplace bullying increase, so does the degree to which the workplace becomes an unsafe place for the people who are bullied and for those who observe what is happening and worry that they might be next in line.

Some people need only witness one of their colleagues bullying another colleague once, to experience their workplace as changed forever. Others may have a higher threshold for observing episodes of workplace bullying before they feel personally compromised by the incidents they witness. People who have been bullied, or who are currently being bullied, often feel betrayed by their employing organization. They find it inexcusable that senior managers who know about the issues they are facing can fail to confront the bullies and require them to stop using abusive behavior in the workplace.

So, what does the phrase 'workplace bullying' conjure up for you? You might like to take a few minutes to jot down in the space below any phrases and words which come to mind when you consider the term 'workplace bullying':

WORKPLACE BULLYING: A DEFINITION

Whatever you have written, and however skeptically or pragmatically you view workplace bullying, you may have had difficulty describing it with any degree of certainty. Consider the following three-part definition which I have developed to capture the key elements – for me at least – of the term 'workplace bullying'.

Workplace bullying is about:

- A personalized, often sustained attack on one colleague by another colleague using behaviors which are emotionally and psychologically punishing.
- Introducing a dynamic into a workplace relationship which involves a purposed attempt by one colleague to injure another colleague's self-esteem, self-confidence and reputation or to undermine their competence to carry out their work duties effectively.
- The degree to which the person using bullying behavior chooses to handle their relationship with a colleague in a way that *involves removing power from their colleague* and placing it with themselves.

The fact that the person using bullying behavior may have organizational authority over the person they are bullying does not justify their behavior. Using a bullying approach is never an alternative to effective management or leadership and the two things should never be confused. The starting point for handling bullying behavior – even if the person using it is senior to you at work – is to realize that the behaviors they employ, and the attitudes they use to justify using those behaviors, are not excusable and do not explain away their interpersonal tactics. Bullying behavior is unjustifiably aggressive behavior which mistreats and harms colleagues.

THE INTENTIONS OF WORKPLACE BULLIES

The intention of the workplace bully is twofold. Firstly, to select a colleague against whom they will mount a personalized campaign; and secondly, to employ a range of behavioral tactics which might result in coworkers joining in that campaign either because they are duped into doing so or because it serves their individual interests to do so. Some bullies are satisfied with doing the first of these two things only. Their intention in mounting a personalized, sustained attack on a colleague is to undermine them by variously:

- Injuring their self-esteem.
- Taking actions which will result in the quality of their colleague's work being lowered.
- Reducing their self-confidence.
- Setting them up to fail in key workplace assignments.
- Excluding them from workplace groups such as decision-making or information-giving forums.
- Discrediting them in the eyes of their coworkers.
- Undermining their reputation at work personally and professionally.
- Reducing their influence and credibility at work.
- Scapegoating them for errors and mistakes they have not committed and/or are not responsible for.
- Galvanizing coworkers into thinking less of them, removing active support from them and/or leaving them out of workplace social events.

Being subject to an attack of this kind can be devastating. Quite often the colleague selected for this treatment is unaware of the true motivation of the bully at the time the campaign begins. Some people have worked comfortably alongside a bully for years before that colleague starts to use bullying behavior out of the blue. Many people subject to workplace bullying wrongly assume that they *have* made an error, or *have* overlooked something important or *deserve* some of the flak they are getting. Others expend energy, time and effort worrying, trying to identify what it was they've done wrong and trying to identify what actions they've taken that could have provoked such aggression. Invariably they can't find very much at all and sometimes they can't find anything at all.

Either way, being on the receiving end of this kind of attack can leave the person subject to it reeling. They feel confused, alone and full of self-doubt. These experiences can be especially debilitating for someone who is not used to feeling these emotions. We will be looking in more detail at the range of emotional and physical consequences that people subject to workplace bullying experience later on in the book, but for now, it is enough for you to know that the impact of workplace bullying on the person being attacked can, in some cases, injure them to the point that they suffer a breakdown and don't easily recover.

BEHAVIORS FREQUENTLY USED BY BULLIES

So far we have been examining what workplace bullying is and describing the underlying intent and motivation of the workplace bully. Let's now look at the range of behaviors that workplace bullies employ. There are many, many behaviors which, given the definition of workplace bullying presented above, fit the bill. Remember that the measure of whether a particular behavior does or does not constitute an example of workplace bullying lies with the *motivation* of the bully in employing that behavior. It is important here to make a distinction between isolated instances – justifiable or unjustifiable – of one colleague being angry with another colleague and the systematic, ongoing, personalized assault that is workplace bullying.

Consider the following categories of behavioral tactics often employed by people using bullying behavior at work, some of which are adapted from work done by the University of Ballarat, Australia:

Verbal Bullying Tactics

- Repeatedly calling a colleague by an insulting name – or repeatedly using a nickname they find offensive or dislike – to refer to them either behind their back, to their face or both.
- Talking about a colleague's performance, character or conduct behind their back for the purpose of discrediting them in the eyes of their colleagues.
- Making verbally abusive comments or remarks about a colleague either in their earshot or behind their back.
- Repeatedly using verbal aggression, shouting or swearing when speaking with a colleague.
- Identifying a colleague's mistake, discussing it in public and over-stating their error for the purpose of discrediting them.
- Deliberately choosing to reprimand, put down or insult a colleague in front of their coworkers.

Nonverbal Bullying Tactics

- Using nonverbal signals that denote disapproval or contempt either for a colleague's presence or for their verbal input, such as rolling one's eyes, continually staring and laughing at what they say whether or not they have made a mistake.

■ Repeatedly using nonverbal aggression such as adopting a threatening posture, clenching their fists or glaring at them when speaking with a colleague.

Practical Bullying Tactics

■ Meddling with a colleague's personal possessions or office property such as knocking the pot plant on their desk onto the floor, removing or hiding their folders or files, using their computer without their permission.

■ Using practical jokes to offend or humiliate a colleague in front of their coworkers.

■ Transmitting nasty or insulting text messages, faxes or e-mails to a colleague or leaving unpleasant messages on their voice mail system.

Performance-related Bullying Tactics

■ Continual unwarranted criticism of a colleague's performance or workplace conduct: in some cases the criticisms are specific and in others they are vague and unclear.

■ Allocating an unreasonable amount of work to a colleague with the intention of setting them up to fail.

■ Purposefully withholding information that a colleague needs to be able to perform effectively in their role; again to set them up to fail.

■ Suggesting overtly or through implication that a colleague's position is under review, that their employment may be terminated or that they may be demoted for the purpose of undermining them.

■ Suggesting overtly or through implication that a colleague will receive a poor appraisal or performance evaluation for the purpose of undermining them.

■ Suggesting overtly or through implication that a colleague's pay or work hours are under review, or that they won't get a particular new role again for the purpose of undermining them.

■ Selectively applying onerous or petty work rules to one colleague but not others to increase the degree of difficulty involved in the first colleague's work and so set them up to fail.

■ Arranging a meeting at a time that is unworkable for a colleague for the purpose of excluding them from the discussion.

- Persistently ignoring the verbal input of a colleague at a meeting or always disagreeing with it.

These categories and the items in them are not meant to be exhaustive but they do fairly represent the range of tactics that people using bullying behavior employ. Each bully will have their own unique motivations for and methods of bullying. The categories and items above represent some of the more commonly used methods of intimidating colleagues and will give you a starting point for assessing whether or not someone you work with is or is not using bullying behavior.

However, it is important to remember that some of the behaviors listed above could be used by your colleagues – or you – quite innocently and, in these cases, would not constitute examples of workplace bullying. For example, it is quite possible for one colleague to forget to tell another colleague an important piece of information which is crucial for their work. The absence of this piece of information may ultimately render the second colleague's work below par. But, the standard for whether the omission of the information constitutes workplace bullying is what the intention of the first colleague was in failing to relay it. If it was simply a matter of having overlooked it, perhaps through being overworked themselves, through being unwell or through simple forgetfulness, that is one thing. But to fail to pass on the information purposefully in order to undermine the quality of work a colleague is doing, and as part of an ongoing campaign against that colleague, is quite another.

Example One: An Incident of Workplace Bullying?

A leading researcher into modern uses for ancient herbal remedies is commissioned to write a book on traditional herbal cures for everyday illnesses by a small publishing company. The publishing company is owned and managed by a man in his mid-50s who, while an able and successful independent publisher, has little confidence in dealing with authors over the telephone and has a strong preference for making all the decisions which pertain to a publication himself. In approaching the researcher he is aware that he is breaking one of his cardinal rules: that of only offering to publish work written by authors he had already met or has worked with previously.

He finds working with the researcher stressful. She has definite views about most aspects of the layout, presentation and marketing of the book, and many of her views do not coincide with his. Rather than welcome her input the publisher begins to cut her out of the decisions that need to be made, making them unilaterally and subsequently informing her about them via e-mail. The researcher is undeterred by this approach and continues to make her opinions known to the publisher after receiving and reading his e-mails. On two occasions she suggests that he overturn his initial decision and replace it with a more rounded and better thought out decision, one which she has already determined. The publisher becomes more and more angry at what he sees as unwarranted interference by the researcher, and begins sending her snide and offhand e-mails. On one occasion he leaves a rude and preemptory message on her voice message system telling her she had better leave the adult decisions to him. The researcher cannot understand why the publisher is treating her in this way and assumes that he is either overworked or going through a bad patch. She has enjoyed working on the production of the book and regards their joint piece of work as one which will create income for him and useful marketing opportunity and publicity for her. She decides that he is tired or stressed and tells herself that it'll all blow over. The researcher looks forward to meeting the publisher face-to-face at the forthcoming alternative medicine fair which they are both attending.

The publisher has arranged to take a stall at the alternative medicine fair so that he can market and sell the book and other related publications that he wants to promote. He arrives before the researcher, sets out his stall and displays ten copies of her book prominently. When the researcher arrives, she goes straight to his stall and introduces herself to him. He pointedly ignores her, carries on with his unpacking and then abruptly walks away toward the coffee stand. He purchases a coffee and returns to the stall to carry on with his unpacking, again ignoring the researcher who is patiently waiting for him to return. She tries to speak with him again, holds out her hand ready to shake his and says hello, calling the publisher by his name and using a warm and friendly tone. The publisher looks up from his boxes and unpacking work, glares at the researcher, brushes her hand aside and tells her in a cold and angry tone that he is too busy to deal with irrelevant people. The researcher is amazed at being spoken to like this and feels humiliated. She gets the message and moves away, disturbed and upset by what she sees as unkindness and unnecessary rudeness.

An Incident of Workplace Bullying?: Analyzing the Dynamics

Let's take a look at what happened in this example to determine whether or not the publisher's treatment of the researcher constitutes workplace bullying or whether it is simply an example of extremely difficult workplace behavior which does not, in and of itself, constitute work-place bullying. To help us make this distinction let's refer back to the three aspects of the definition of workplace bullying introduced at the start of the chapter. In order for the publisher's conduct to constitute workplace bullying it must satisfy all three criteria simultaneously.

Firstly, does the behavior of the publisher involve using psycho-logically and emotionally punishing behavior toward the researcher? Certainly it does. His behavior is rude, dismissive, derisory and unrea-sonable and the researcher quite understandably feels hurt and upset by it. Moreover she cannot account for why the publisher treats her the way he does when they are collaborating together on a piece of work which will bring them both benefits.

Secondly, does the publisher introduce a dynamic into his relation-ship with the researcher which involves a purposed attempt by him to injure her self-esteem and self-confidence or to undermine her compe-tence to carry out her work? No, he does not. His intention in using the behavior he chooses when dealing with the researcher is not spe-cifically to upset or injure her, although it is inevitable that he will do so. His aim is to retain control of the decision-making process around the publication of the book she has written, and to dissuade her from offering further input to that process. He wants to make all the deci-sions surrounding the publication of the book himself, unilaterally, and to subsequently inform her of them by e-mail. He wants her to simply accept them without questioning them or commenting on them and when she proves unwilling to do so, and worse, questions his judgement by providing alternative ways forward, he employs punish-ing tactics to try and get her to cease offering unwanted points of view. The publisher has a very high need for control and cannot cope with what he sees as the researcher's interference in his business. He does not recognize that she has a right to provide input to decisions about a book that she wrote. Nor does he recognize that she might have valuable perspectives to offer him on how to go about marketing and promoting the book. He has a strong preference for working alone and is ruthless in his pursuit of his right to work this way. However, his motivation is not consistent with that of a workplace bully because the goal he is pursuing is simply to get back to a situation where he and he alone is the one calling the shots and making the decisions. It is not to undermine the work, self-esteem or self-confidence of the researcher, although his tactics could certainly result in some or all of these outcomes.

Thirdly, does the publisher choose to handle his relationship with the researcher in a way that *involves removing power from her* and placing it with himself? Yes he does, but only with regards to the decision-making processes around the layout, presentation and marketing of the book and not in relation to any other aspects of his relationship with her. For instance, he does not try and influence what she writes in the book. Nor does he replace the words she has written with his, once she hands the book typescript over to him. So, while he does make a series of decisions without input from the researcher and subsequently ignores her unwanted input – thereby denying her any power in the decision-making processes around the publication of the book – the publisher's actions do not represent a consistent attempt to remove personal power from the researcher and place it with him and so do not constitute outright workplace bullying.

An Incident of Workplace Bullying?: Conclusions

So what conclusions can we draw from this example? The publisher uses unjustifiable aggression toward the researcher because he lacks the interpersonal skills and resolve to handle his own anger at having, as he sees it, his judgement questioned by her. He lacks the maturity, sensitivity or conflict-handling skills to do so. By the time of the alternative medicine fair his only mode when dealing with the researcher is a rude, aggressive and demeaning one. But it is not characterized by a sustained attack on her for the purposes of discrediting her or her work, or of undermining her competence to do her job. Most likely, the publisher will not need to contact the researcher again after the alternative medicine fair and there will be no more incidents of his unpleasant behavior toward her. None of this excuses the publisher at all. He employs thoroughly reprehensible behavior with someone he sought out to work with. However, it probably does absolve him from being a workplace bully.

From the researcher's point of view, she is not in an ongoing workplace relationship with the publisher, doesn't really need to keep in contact with him once the book has been produced and can walk away from the business relationship at any time she wants. His behavior toward her does not affect anyone else's view of her and so is not divisive no matter how difficult it is for her to deal with. For our purposes then, no matter how problematic and upsetting his approach is to the researcher, the publisher's behavior is not an example of workplace bullying, but is an example of dishonorable and unjustified aggression against a workplace contact.

So if the publisher's behavior does not constitute workplace bullying, what does?

Example Two: Bullying in the Workplace

A software design company hires a new CAD operator to join an existing team of six people. The new operator is replacing a popular and long-standing member of the workforce who decided to emigrate with her husband upon his retirement. On her first day at work the new CAD operator is surprised to find that her desk is situated away from the other six members of the team in a cramped space close to the noisy lift shaft which serves the upper floors of the building. On her first day the new CAD operator is introduced by the team manager to the existing six members of the team, who are all seated at a row of desks on the other side of the room. While one of them comes over and shakes her hand warmly the rest merely look up from their work to regard her unsmilingly before turning back to their computers without speaking to her or returning her greeting. One person in particular looks at her with a mean expression and is the last to turn back to her desk without talking to her.

Over the next few days the CAD operator starts to feel distinctly uncomfortable. She notices that her colleagues go to lunch in twos and threes but do not include her in their plans. She notices that they make cups of tea and coffee for one another but do not offer to make a cup for her at the same time. On two occasions she approaches the bank of computers where her team colleagues are seated to ask questions about company procedures on various matters. No one responds to her verbal request for information and she is forced to return, defeated and embarrassed, to her desk.

After three days her manager calls her to his office and asks her how she is settling in. She says that she would prefer to be seated with the other members of the team. The manager says he will see what he can do and will get back to her when he has considered the logistics involved in relocating her workstation alongside the other desks. Later that afternoon, she notices him speaking with the rest of the team by their desks. She hopes that he is discussing how to situate her desk near theirs. When he calls her into his office just as she is leaving at the end of the day, she is dismayed to learn that the rest of the team don't think there is enough space on their side of the room to accommodate her and believe it would be better to leave the desks arranged as they currently are.

Over the next two weeks the new CAD operator becomes more and more concerned about the situation she finds herself in. Firstly, she realizes that she is routinely being left out of e-mail exchanges originated by her team colleagues, e-mail exchanges which affect the whole team and should be circulated to her as well. On one occasion she realizes that she has been omitted from all the replies to an e-mail thread she had initiated. Secondly, she starts to worry that the other members of the team are talking about her behind her back. Not usually given to a suspicious turn of mind she initially dismisses these thoughts as nonsense, despite noticing that whispered conversations and huddles seem to break up whenever she enters the room and seem to start as she leaves it. She is particularly concerned to note that one person is always involved in these gossipy cliques: the colleague who looked at her with the most obvious distaste on being introduced to her on her first day. Thirdly, she attends the Friday morning team meeting at the end of her second week and, during a planned section on customer service improvements, makes the suggestion that team members not involved in a phone call can take their time responding to new incoming calls. Three team members, including the most unpleasant of her colleagues, snigger at her remark and the unpleasant colleague subsequently refers to her as 'miss goody two shoes', a comment which results in further laughter at her expense.

The new CAD operator has not experienced a workplace like this one before and has no previous experiences of being treated like this by coworkers. She is particularly concerned that her team manager, who was present at the Friday morning meeting, seems to be absenting himself from doing anything about the situation; and that even the person who was welcoming to her on her first morning has now joined her other five team colleagues in their treatment of her. She starts to feel that she has made a big mistake in joining this company. By the start of her third week of employment she sleeps less well, begins to lose her appetite and starts to make small, but increasingly numerous, errors in her work.

After five weeks she makes a more serious error, one that could have been avoided had she felt able to approach either her manager or her team colleagues and ask them a question about the joint project she is working on. She didn't approach her team members, afraid that had she done so, they would either have ignored her or would have used her lack of knowledge as an opportunity to ridicule her and laugh at her. She didn't approach her team manager because she sees him as unsupportive and as someone who regards her colleagues' behavior toward her as irrelevant and unimportant. She therefore doesn't trust him.

Unfortunately, her error causes the client for whom she is working to make a complaint to her manager. Her manager calls the new CAD operator into his office and explains the situation to her. He is not unkind but is firm and clear. He tells her that she cannot afford to make serious errors like this one. The CAD operator tells him that she is being picked on and undermined by her coworkers and that he must have noticed. He replies by saying that they are just having a bit of harmless fun and she shouldn't be so sensitive. Then he tells her in a weary voice that she's taking it personally and that they treat every new employee like this. The new CAD operator knows that this isn't true. Apart from her, no one else has been hired into the department for years. She leaves his office dismayed at his attitude, feeling isolated and alone, and concerned that she doesn't have anyone at work to turn to who will listen to her or do anything to support her.

Bullying in the Workplace: Analyzing the Dynamics

Let's take a look at what happened in this example to determine whether or not the CAD team's treatment of their new colleague constitutes workplace bullying. To help us make this distinction let's refer back to the three aspects of the definition of workplace bullying introduced at the start of the chapter.

Firstly, does the behavior of the existing CAD team members involve using psychologically and emotionally punishing behavior toward their new colleague? Certainly it does. From the first moments of being introduced to her the existing CAD team members treat her with disdain, and refuse to display even common courtesy toward her by saying hello or acknowledging her presence. Over the next few weeks their tactics against her escalate so that different members of the existing CAD team are variously guilty of:

- Excluding their new colleague from normal office conversations, social arrangements and informal get togethers.
- Refusing to allow her to situate her desk near theirs.
- Cutting her out of e-mail strings, even ones she has originated.
- Gossiping about her as she leaves the office.
- Using her entrance to the office as an opportunity to alienate her further by ceasing to have whispered, giggly chats – a move which naturally leaves her questioning whether or not they were talking about her behind her back.
- Calling her by a demeaning nickname at a team meeting and characterizing her attempt to improve response times to incoming calls as an example of her being a goody-goody.

Secondly, do the existing CAD team members introduce a dynamic into their relationship with their new colleague which involves a purposed attempt by them to injure her self-esteem and self-confidence or to undermine her competence to carry out her work? Certainly they do. They laugh at her, ridicule her, ignore her, exclude her, gossip about her, cause her to worry that they might be gossiping about her and leave her in no doubt that she is outside their group and the object of its derision. The one member of the team who does say hello to her on her first day quickly changes her stance and joins the clique that appears to be led by the team member who is most unpleasant to the new CAD operator on meeting her. All these issues affect both her self-esteem and her self-confidence. They also affect her standard of work. She is unable to carry out her part of the work on a joint project to the required standard without the input of her team colleagues; and she fails to solicit that input because she fears being humiliated again. Their active campaign against her directly results in her making an error serious enough for her client to issue a complaint about her and for her manager to feel the need to intervene. Overall, the treatment she receives from the existing CAD team members affects her morale, her appetite and her sleep, causing her to doubt herself and feel alienated at work. It negatively impacts her self-esteem, self-confidence and her competence to carry out her work duties.

Thirdly, do the existing CAD team members choose to handle their relationship with their new colleague in a way that *involves removing power from her* and placing it with themselves? Absolutely they do. The new colleague has no power at all in her workplace. She never gains any influence at work because she doesn't have any functioning workplace relationships. She doesn't have any functioning workplace relationships because she is denied the opportunity to develop any through her team colleagues' conduct toward her. They want her to feel isolated, friendless and alone at work. They achieve this aim through their joint involvement in a campaign of workplace intimidation and gossiping; and by deliberately excluding their colleague from the normal life of the workplace.

Bullying in the Workplace: Conclusions

What conclusions can we draw from this example? In the situation described above, a new employee is bullied from day one of her employment and can have no inkling of the kind of reception she is in for. Neither can she have done anything to provoke, justify or preempt such treatment. Her livelihood depends on her carrying out her new role effectively and she is not prepared for the ruthless campaign that is carried out against her by her new colleagues.

The manager of the CAD team is complicit in enabling this situation by failing to see the bullying behavior for what it is. He ignores it, doesn't take it seriously at all and enables it by failing to confront it. Even when the bullying is carried out at a team meeting right under his nose, the manager fails to engage with the bullying behavior and subsequently adds insult to injury by blaming his new team member for 'taking it personally'.

The workplace bullying to which she is subject seems to be orchestrated by one particularly unpleasant existing CAD team member. This person succeeds in crystallizing her colleagues' latent and unfounded animosity toward their new colleague into an active campaign against her. Everyone of the existing CAD team eventually participates actively in this campaign, even the person who initially was warm and welcoming toward the new team member. Having been rendered powerless at work, unless her situation improves quickly, the new CAD team member will most likely experience a further deterioration in the standard of her work, and her mental and physical well-being.

We will be looking in detail at what factors cause people to use bullying behavior at work – and to inspire others to join them in this activity – in the following chapter. For now, it is enough to say that one of the features that makes workplace bullying so divisive is how difficult it is for an employee to walk away from the bullying because that inevitably means walking away from their job and their income. This is no easy thing to do at the best of times, but is particularly challenging for someone whose self-belief has taken a battering following an experience of workplace bullying – and who realizes that no one around them seems to take what is happening to them seriously enough to do anything about it.

YOUR GOAL IN RESPONDING
TO WORKPLACE BULLYING

Many people affected by workplace bullying are bewildered by the experience. It often comes out of the blue and, being unexpected, can leave them shaken and flatfooted or simply overwhelmed right from the off. Some people subject to workplace bullying are so disorientated by the unforeseen aggression they receive that they are defeated by it before they've had time to assimilate what is happening to them. Others recognize it for what it is but simply don't know how to deal with such a relentless, personalized attack having had neither the training in how to do so nor a similar experience from which to draw effective lessons.

Should you be subject to workplace bullying you may find it difficult to respond effectively early enough in the experience of being bullied to protect yourself – and some of you may be unable to respond effectively at all. The psychological mugging which happens when you find that sudden, unexpected aggression is used against you in your place of work can leave you paralyzed by fear, self-doubt, confusion and sometimes, sadly, also shame. My hope is that this book will help those of you who are yet to be bullied at work, and those of you early on in an experience of workplace bullying, to find a way of responding effectively to bullying behaviors as and when they happen; and that it will help others of you to haul back some of the personal power and self-confidence you have already lost through being subject to ongoing workplace bullying.

My goal is to equip you with the insight, knowledge, interpersonal strategies and intrapersonal awareness that will enable you to respond to bullying behavior by:

- Appropriately defending your self-esteem, self-confidence and emotional or psychological well-being.
- Preserving your personal power and personal boundaries, thus protecting your inner self.
- Handling the bullying behavior at the time it occurs so that you retain control of the situation as much as possible and demonstrate to the bully that their tactics will not prevail against you in the long run.

SUMMARY AND NEXT CHAPTER

This chapter has set the scene for the rest of the book which will focus on how to identify, handle and manage bullying behavior in the workplace. The chapter has included:

- An opportunity for you to outline what 'workplace bullying' means to you.
- A three-stage definition of workplace bullying.
- A discussion of the intentions and motivations of workplace bullies.
- Two examples which make a distinction between unreasonable workplace aggression and behavior which constitutes workplace bullying.
- An outline of the goals you might like to work toward should you be subject to workplace bullying.

The next chapter will focus in some detail on the factors and intrapersonal dynamics that cause people to start using bullying behavior at work.

CHAPTER 2

Why People Bully Their Colleagues
The Psychological Profile of a Workplace Bully

It is time now to take a detailed look at the people who use bullying behavior at work. In this chapter we will:

- Examine why people start to bully their colleagues.
- Identify a range of intrapersonal factors which can result in a person becoming a workplace bully.
- Consider a range of factors that people who use bullying behavior cite to justify their behavior.
- Identify some of the euphemisms and excuses bullies – and some of their colleagues – use to reduce their behavior to something more acceptable.
- Take a look at why it is that some bullies can inspire other colleagues to join in their campaign against selected individuals.

In all of these discussions it is important to note that every bully is unique and has their own intrapersonal and situational context for using bullying behavior. Equally, every bullying relationship is different and has its own dynamic. I'd like us to avoid making generalizations and, with this in mind, let's start by examining the disposition of people likely to become – or who have already become – workplace bullies.

THE DISPOSITION OF THE WORKPLACE BULLY

While it is probably true to say that, at some time or the other in their working life, just about anyone could become the target – whether successful or unsuccessful – of a workplace bully, it is not true to say that just about anyone could start to use bullying behavior in the workplace. You'd have to want to handle your workplace relationships in this way. You'd have to want to use intimidating and dominating behavior with your colleagues. Or, at the very least, you'd have to be willing to accept that the actions you take while using bullying behavior with a colleague – no matter how pressurizing, unreasonable and forceful – were either:

- Necessary
- Imperative
- Justifiable
- Deserved
- Or didn't really hurt anyone

The choice to bully a colleague comes out of intrapersonal and situational factors that result in the bully using unreasonable, persistent aggression against selected workplace targets. Every bully has their own, unique reasons for using bullying behavior. In their minds, people who use bullying behavior may well regard their actions as:

- Necessary because they think that without their input their department will fail to meet its targets.
- Imperative because they fear that they are not as good at their job as the colleague they are targeting is at theirs – and they need to create enough camouflage so that their own shortcomings are hidden.
- Justifiable because they consider that the people they target are under-performing and need to be kicked into gear.
- Deserved because if the people they target don't start performing *they* will be deemed to have failed – a situation they cannot tolerate.
- Blameless because they don't consciously intend to hurt anyone and don't really believe that their actions will cause harm to their colleagues.

Let's illustrate these issues by examining three Character Cameos. Each of the cameos focuses on a different set of factors behind a manager's decision to use bullying behavior at work. Each of the three managers has a different intrapersonal context for their decision to bully and also a different set of challenging workplace issues to handle. While it is true that the majority of workplace bullies are managers who bully their team members, it is also true, as we saw in the first chapter, that peers can bully one another and, on occasion , that team members can bully their bosses.

Let's consider character cameo one:

Character Cameo One: The Threatened Senior Manager

A small PR consultancy decides to expand. All four of its existing, overworked employees agree that growing the business is both desirable and necessary. Currently the Chairman, his PA and his two consultants carry out all the duties needed to keep the business running smoothly but the three fee earners regularly complain to one another that they don't have enough time to focus as fully as they'd like to on finding and working with clients.

After a lengthy recruitment process they hire an assertive young man in his mid-20s who has the necessary qualifications to work in the firm but no prior experience. They offer him a six-month probationary contract with a view to a permanent position should his performance during those six months come up to scratch. The firm's aim is to invest in his development for half a year, assess his appetite and capacity for the work and groom him to become the fourth fee earner. With this in mind they set him the informal target of earning some income for the firm by the end of that period. The Chairman tells him that earning fees by the end of his probation period is not a precondition to him being offered a permanent contract, but it does give him something concrete to aim for and should be taken as a sign of the firm's faith in his untapped potential. He is both pleased and excited at the challenge. He accepts the offer and thinks he will fit into the firm just fine.

The Chairman tells him that his manager will be one of the two existing fee earners at the firm, a woman in her 40s who has been with the company since it was formed. They get on well during the new employee's first few weeks with the firm, and the new recruit proves to be a popular and well-liked addition to the workforce. The new recruit finds his new manager to be systematic, methodical, detailed and someone who likes advance notice of the issues involved before making a decision. He appreciates her willingness to take time to explain and coach him, but finds her style somewhat inflexible and a touch controlling. However, he readily approaches her with questions and queries and gets a lot out of his manager's experience and willingness to invest time in him. After three months of working together, however, and just as the new recruit is starting to make real progress, things start to change.

The new recruit is given a small but important account to manage but is told that he must run all his decisions past his manager before implementing them. He arranges to meet his new client and tells his manager about the agenda and outcomes he wants to pursue at the meeting. His manager decides to invite herself along to the meeting and, when the new recruit is disappointed, dismisses him with a curt: 'You're too inexperienced. You need an older head there.' The new recruit does all the spadework for the meeting which does go well, but at which the manager does all the talking. After the meeting she expects the new recruit to document the outputs of the meeting and work single-handedly on the design of the PR campaign for the client.

During the following week the manager's tone and style of handling the new recruit continue to become more and more unreasonable. She complains loudly when her younger colleague is nine minutes late one morning. Despite assuring his boss that he'd gladly stay late to make up the time, the older manager doesn't cease complaining, and in fact even mentions to the Chairman later that day that she thinks their new recruit will be prone to laziness if she doesn't keep on top of him. The following week the manager organizes an impromptu Status Update Meeting and grills the new recruit on his handling of the client assignment he is near to completing. He has worked hard on the PR campaign and put both thought and application into it. All he hears from his manager during the update meeting is a series of pointed, picky questions and critical comments which leave him cross and drain his enthusiasm.

The tone of the meeting also troubles him: it is as if his manager simply wants someone to take her growing irritation and bad temper out on. At no stage does she listen to or seek to work constructively with the new recruit. At no stage does she verbally recognize how much effort and work her younger colleague has put into the project. In fact her approach throughout is punitive, heckling and snide.

Two days later the new recruit is dismayed to learn that his manager has arranged a meeting with his client behind his back and hasn't invited him to it. He walks into her office to confront her and asks why she has arranged a meeting with his client on his account, why he wasn't included in that decision and why he hasn't been invited to that meeting. His boss turns slowly around in her chair to face her colleague and tells him in even tones that he can't expect to be included in key client-facing decisions if his work isn't up to scratch. The new recruit asks in what way his work isn't up to scratch and receives the frosty reply: 'I spent time taking you through all that yesterday.' The new recruit tries to defend himself explaining, with a growing sense of panic and desperation, that he has worked hard on the account, has done good work on the account and isn't being treated fairly. His manager, smooth and commanding, tells him that she hasn't got time to take him through it all again, and perhaps he'd like to review his notes. She also points out that she is earning the fees that pay her younger colleague's salary and needs to get on with her work.

Later that day she arranges a meeting with the Chairman. She tells him that the new recruit is struggling to handle the responsibility of the account he is managing and that she'd like to support him. She explains that she will be accompanying him to the next client meeting. She reminds the Chairman of the need for the new recruit to start to earn fees before the end of his probationary period and suggests, in a sympathetic tone, that it might not work out if she, the senior player, doesn't keep an eye on him. The Chairman replies by encouraging the consultant to do just that and thanking her for her time and enthusiasm in developing their new colleague.

* * *

Having taken a look at the action let's now analyze what is going on in the mind of the consultant that would account for her bullying behavior toward her younger colleague. The following section will take you behind her interpersonal conduct and into her intrapersonal world. It will clarify the links between her inner, intrapersonal landscape and her subsequent interpersonal behavior.

Character Cameo One: The Intrapersonal World of the Consultant

At the start of the action the consultant is keen to recruit a new member to the workforce, genuinely pleased at the prospect of securing the services of such a high potential, if untried, new recruit and pleased to be chosen as the one to manage and coach him. She is a methodical and logical woman, someone who values order, structure and precision in her work and who has a higher than average need to control. None of these things precludes her being an effective manager or mentor to the new recruit and, although he finds his new boss's style somewhat awkward, the new recruit adapts enough to the work preferences of his manager that he enjoys working with her and makes rapid progress.

However, after three months there is a discernible change in her manager's attitude toward her younger colleague that the junior consultant neither anticipates nor correctly interprets. So what is happening in the inner world of the manager that could account for her sudden frosty and duplicitous behavior? Her change of internal temperature causes her to:

- Give unnecessarily destructive, biased and negative feedback to the new recruit over his work on his first account.
- Undermine her younger colleague's confidence and self-esteem by overlooking the many strengths of his work on that project.

- Step in to arrange a meeting with her young colleague's client, leaving him out of the communication loop and meeting.
- Tell him that his work isn't up to scratch but provide no evidence or rationale for this claim when subsequently asked to elaborate.
- Remind her younger colleague that *she* is earning the money that keeps the new recruit in his role.
- Go behind his back and suggest to the Chairman that the new recruit needs her support if he is to make the grade.

What can account for this behavior? Basically, after working with him for a few months, the consultant begins to feel threatened by her new recruit. Instead of taking the view that he represents exactly what the *company* needs – an energetic, bright, confident and able new member of the team – she starts to feel *personally* threatened that her younger colleague might prove more able than she is. She envies her colleague's popularity around the office, his spontaneous and easy way with people, his apparent lack of fear at the six-month timeline for earning fees. She feels slighted that her effort and time in coaching her new recruit seems to be leading to kudos for her younger colleague but not for her. She starts to feel unappreciated even though her younger colleague clearly does appreciate his manager's time and application in coaching him. She looks at her colleague and then at herself and sees herself as the less able of the two, the less effective, the less socially able and, potentially, the less useful member of the workforce. She feels scared.

Rather than confront her own jealousy and envy or her fears about her competency or future with the firm, she decides that she must bring her younger colleague down to prevent him from proving himself to be better at his job than she is at hers. She starts to undermine him, finds fault with his work and exaggerates the small errors and learning opportunities she does find in his work into much more grievous issues than they actually are.

Unfortunately no one else in the firm notices what is happening. In public and around her other colleagues the consultant presents herself as supportive toward the new recruit. She appears sympathetic toward his steep learning curve and optimistic about his progress. But, in private, she whispers that he might be slacking and mightn't make the grade. She plays on her established relationship with the Chairman to manage his perceptions of the new recruit so that, at some time down the road, should she need to play her trump card and suggest they terminate his employment, she will already have sown seeds of doubt into the minds of her senior colleague about the effectiveness and conduct of the new recruit.

The consultant's impulse to destroy her opponent, as she sees it, is both primitive and vicious. Her fear, jealousy and envy are no defense for her behavior: they are the problem. Her jealousy results in her wanting to destroy the reputation, character and standing that her younger colleague has earned through his hard work and admirable conduct since joining the firm; in other words she wants to destroy the good that her colleague has earned and worked for and deprive him of it. Her envy drives her to want to acquire the credit and the rewards that ought rightly to go to her younger colleague and keep them for herself; in other words she wants to take away the good that her colleague has earned and keep it for herself.

Unless she starts to look inward and see her fear, jealousy and envy for what they are, she will continue to blind herself to her real motives and will continue to assail her younger colleague with nit-picky, critical and unfounded negative feedback, while ignoring or overlooking the excellent work he is doing. She will continue to use insidious and manipulative tactics to damage her colleague's reputation with the firm's Chairman, and continue to undermine her younger colleague's self-confidence and self-esteem. Equally, unless the new recruit starts to see his boss's behavior for what it is and begins to redress the damage done to his reputation in the firm quickly and effectively he may find that, for all his endeavor and learning, his contract may be in doubt at the end of the six-month period. He is particularly vulnerable to this happening as he isn't working day to day with anyone other than his manager. Without anyone else to vouch for the quality of his *work* – as opposed to his popularity around the office which everyone can clearly see – he is on a sticky wicket.

* * *

We have just examined an instance of a person's fear, jealousy and envy resulting in them seeing a new colleague as a threat and leading them to employ bullying behavior against that colleague. Let's now look at a second instance of workplace bullying, one which occurs for very different reasons than those described above.

Character Cameo Two: Switch of Roles

A large firm of accountants moves one of its top performing managers from the department he successfully runs to head a separate newly formed department. The department he leaves is highly structured, with set processes and procedures which facilitate the flow of work. The manager has worked there for seven years before his transfer to the new department and during all of that time reported to one Partner with whom he developed a close and effective working relationship.

During his time in that role he gained a reputation as a thorough and competent manager. He is put in charge of the newly formed department and given responsibility for running it from day one. He is energized by the appointment, regards it as a testament to his track record of delivering on time and to standard and, in advance of taking up his new post, he starts to assemble his team. He hires two people from outside the firm and recruits all the rest of his people from existing departments until he has a team of ten people ready and able to work with him from the first day of the new department's work. He meets with his new manager, a different Partner, and they agree that the Partner will adopt a hands-off approach to give the newly promoted manager time to settle in and run things his way.

Two months into his new role things are not going well for him. He struggles to set goals for his team members or clarify direction for the department, issues which, in his previous role, were taken care of for him by the highly structured working environment and the Partner to whom he reported. He won't admit to himself that he is struggling to handle his new set of responsibilities, and it doesn't occur to him to seek development in the skills he needs to enable him to set direction for the department and coach his team members toward their goals. His normal relaxed and informal style is replaced by a harassed and irritable demeanor, and he starts to point out errors and inefficiencies in his team members' work in a peevish and blaming tone. Rather than recognize that the issues the department is facing lie with him, he starts to micromanage his team. He dives in and out of their work, sends them preemptory emails entitled 'Things I'm Concerned About' which list issues that he has with their work, prevents them from attending meetings with clients or with colleagues outside the department and becomes critical and disparaging in his face-to-face dealings with them.

He decides that the only person trying to get anything done in the department is himself. He begins to see his team members as below par. He thinks of them as people who can't stand the pace, people who are weak, mediocre and slow to get things done. He characterizes them as incompetent while all the time regarding himself as capable, active and competent. He lets this view of things show in his dealings with his team members, which results in them feeling dislike for him as a person and mistrust of him as a manager.

One team member tries to reason with him and this proves to be a trigger point in his dealings with her. She comes to see him in his office one Monday morning. Rather than see her well-intentioned attempt to speak with him as kindly meant, he turns on her with ferocious animosity and yells at her: 'How dare you question my competence? It's you lot that aren't up to scratch!' From that moment on he becomes increasingly nasty with her. He blames her – totally irrationally – for not being good enough and for contributing to his current difficulties. He begins to scapegoat her and takes every opportunity to humiliate, undermine, hurt and reduce her. These conversations always take place in private and, although the other members of the team know that they are happening, no one steps in to help her.

The manager is particularly devious in his dealings with this team member. He starts his one-to-one meetings with her with the words: 'I want to work with you, I don't want to undermine you.' This is a very clever tactic that initially throws her off guard, making the following ear bashing all the more damaging. He bombards her with a huge number of top priority pieces of work, tells her that her work is 'crap', doesn't offer her any coaching or support, interrupts and talks over her at their one-to-one meetings and presents himself to her as a world-weary manager tired of the mediocrity around him. The team member tries to reason with him twice but soon realizes that he isn't open to negotiation, isn't going to listen to anyone except himself and has developed fixed and firm views about her supposed incompetence and his supposed superiority over her. She decides to try and tough and it out but, after six further weeks, when she finds that she cannot sleep, she starts to look for another job in another firm.

* * *

Having taken a look at the action let's now analyze what is going on in the mind of the manager that, to him at least, justifies his conduct around the office. The following section will take you behind his interpersonal behavior and into his intrapersonal world. It will clarify the links between his inner, private world and his subsequent behavior toward his team members.

Character Cameo Two: Scapegoating Others

At the start of the action a competent manager with a track record as someone who delivers and runs a tight department is, as he sees it, promoted to a new role. He is excited about his new challenge and takes it as a pat on the back. He gets his team together and they start work but, from early on, there are problems and the manager doesn't get to grips with any of them.

Initially, he fails to realize two key things about his new role: firstly, that he isn't comfortable working in an unstructured environment; and secondly, that he needs someone above him to set direction for him, direction which he then devolves to his team. Without a clear structure within which to work, and without direction set from above, the manager quickly feels overwhelmed by his responsibilities, feels rudderless, fears failing in his new role and fears the humiliation that he would feel should he fail. As an alternative to being honest with himself about his own shortcomings and his growing self-doubt, he starts to deflect blame onto his team members. He decides that *they* are the problem: *they* are failing him, *they* are slow and ineffective, *they* are incompetent.

He decides that he has to manage the perception that the Partners have of his department and its work. One of the first actions he takes is to prevent his team members from attending meetings with colleagues from outside the department or with clients. This maneuver has the effect of:

- Cutting his team members out of information-giving loops in the firm.
- Reducing the influence they have inside and outside of their department.
- Enabling him to manage the perceptions that his senior colleagues have about the quality of work done by the department.
- Opening the way for him to characterize his department and its staff any way he likes to the Partners in the firm.
- Placing him in a position of total control in the department.

Why does he do this? His self-esteem and self-image are predicated on him seeing himself as an effective and successful manager. He simply cannot afford to fail either in his own eyes or in the eyes of his more senior colleagues and he fears that either or both of these outcomes might be possibilities. He decides to baton down the hatches and goes full out to defend himself against the perception by any senior colleague that he and his department are failing. He doesn't address his own development issues; he doesn't learn the management or leadership skills he needs to succeed; he doesn't take advantage of the skills of his team members to help set direction for the department; and he doesn't trust them to work competently and capably. Instead, he sets about managing the perceptions of people outside his department while he uses punishing and scornful behavior with his team members – behavior that, sadly, might mean that some of them are less effective than they'd be if he managed them effectively.

In particular, he singles out one of his team members for special treatment. This person approaches him to speak with him about the issues in the department. She is motivated by concern for him, for herself and for her team colleagues. However, her actions open the team member up to a sustained experience of workplace bullying, an experience which eventually results in her deciding to seek employment elsewhere. Her manager reacts furiously to her carefully worded, calm statement that maybe there are some issues in the department that need to be handled differently. Instead of hearing this as a supportive offer of help, the manager hears it as someone suggesting that he is failing – something that he cannot stand hearing.

He begins a campaign aimed at undermining this team member, a strategy which enables him to deflect his growing feelings of incompetence onto her and characterize her as an inadequate, weak failure in his stead. He wants to make her feel incompetent and uses a well-honed set of skills and tactics by which to achieve this aim. Afraid of the consequences for him of his poor performance as a manager, he uses her as a scapegoat for his failings so that he can deflect attention away from himself and onto her. His fallacious hope is that by deflecting his feelings onto her, and punishing her, he won't feel them anymore and his discomfort will be alleviated. Actually, he is completely wrong. He will still feel the full force of his considerable fear, but now he also has to deal with the fact that his actions cause an able member of the team to look for employment elsewhere, and result in all his other team members mistrusting him even more. Sadly, his actions actually make it more likely that he, and his department, might not succeed in their work, something for which, no matter how skilled he is at managing the Partners' perceptions, he may well pay the ultimate price.

* * *

We have just looked at an example of how a person's desire to scapegoat one colleague in particular, while blaming his entire department for his own shortcomings, results in him using bullying behavior. In this case, the bully mistakenly thinks that the 'cause' of his problems at work lies with his team members in the department when actually it lies fairly and squarely with him.

Let's now examine one more instance of workplace bullying, one which illustrates a third set of circumstances which could result in a person starting to use bullying behavior at work.

Character Cameo Three: Clash of Styles

A 28-year-old technology graduate who has traveled extensively in the Australian outback since leaving university has latterly been working in his father's business. He decides to take on a fresh challenge and is recruited to join the technology group of a global financial institution. He is placed on its fast track Technologists Development Program and is given a twelve-month rotation around four key departments in the technology group. His rotations take him to New York, London, Tokyo and Frankfurt and, after the twelve-month period is up, he moves permanently to London where he is placed in charge of Technology Upgrades for the front office Global Markets team. His role involves managing the replacement of existing hardware and software with new cutting-edge systems that will improve the productivity and response times of the Global Markets traders. The traders are keen to get their hands on the new technology as soon as possible, but are also impatient with what they see as the slow progress being made by the technology team as they implement the upgrade. They variously complain about the unassertive demeanor of the technologists they deal with, their slow and risk-averse working styles and their tendency to block progress rather than facilitate action.

The new Technology Upgrade manager is raw, ambitious and extremely driven. He possesses self-confidence, an appetite for working long hours and sufficient technical knowledge that he is the stand out candidate for the role. His rotation has equipped him with knowledge of the firm, its technology platforms and the demanding nature of the front office traders who work under enormous pressure. He sees his new role as a big opportunity for him to make his name in the technology group. He appreciates just how demanding his client base will be, but doesn't expect that his new team members will have as much trouble dealing with them as they appear to do. During the same week that six key clients come to his office to complain about the way in which their technology colleague is handling his responsibilities, the new Technology Upgrade manager decides that he has to take a different tack with his team. He starts to drive them hard, demanding daily updates from each of them. He begins calling their clients to check on their satisfaction with service and does so without informing his team members about these calls in advance. He is aggressive and pushy in his face-to-face meetings with his team and starts to assume that the most reticent and reserved of his team members might prove incompetent to handle their more robust front office colleagues effectively.

One team member in particular causes him concern. This team member is quiet, restrained and occasionally unforthcoming. He is also an authority on his technical specialism – a specialism that the Technology Upgrade manager isn't proficient in – and has worked for years for the technology group, so far with only positive performance reviews. The manager decides that the best way to manage his team member is to put him under pressure so he calls him into his office and asks him how things are going.

His team member replies that his project is proceeding according to plan, an answer which he delivers in a flat tone and without enthusiasm. This verbal style only serves to further annoy his boss who, after fielding so many client complaints that week, takes a different view. He tells his colleague that he is not satisfied. Asked why, he replies that the team member isn't 'out there' enough, isn't demonstrating to the clients that he is 'on top of it' and comes over 'poorly'. The team member is stunned at the criticisms and the aggression with which they are being conveyed. From his point of view, the project *is* progressing well: it is on time, to specification and standard. He does not understand the feedback and says so, which only serves to annoy his manager even more. The Technology Upgrade manager ignores this response and instead tells his team member in emotional and hostile tones that he expects everyone on his team to pull their weight and that he'll be all over him 'like a rash from now on'. The team member leaves the office shaken. He goes back to his desk and tries to assimilate what he has been told: that his project which is going well isn't going well and that it is because of the way he is doing things.

Over the next week he keeps his head down but starts to feel anxiety every time he sees his manager around the office. He finds it difficult to concentrate and avoids going to speak with his manager about the work issues which he would otherwise like to discuss with him. Everyday his manager comes over to his desk in the open-plan office and, standing over him impatiently with arms folded, asks him for an update on the progress of his project. The flustered team member delivers his progress report as best he can but finds his manager more and more intimidating. He produces less and less output over the rest of the week. Eventually, after a troubled weekend, he requests a move to another group, a request which his manager refuses, claiming that his expert knowledge is needed on the project.

The Technology Upgrade manager keeps up his pressurizing and intrusive management of his team member. He suggests that he undertake assertiveness training and 'toughen up'. He also tells him to 'stop being a chicken' with the front office. The team member feels as if his character, personality and style are under constant scrutiny. They have never been an issue for his previous managers who have always seen him as a safe pair of hands, praising his work ethic, attention to detail and thorough approach. Instead of looking forward to coming to work, and enjoying the responsibility of managing such a high profile project, it isn't long before the team member dreads coming to work and starts to make mistakes which come to the attention of his clients and his boss.

***

Having taken a look at the action let's now analyze what is going on in the mind of the Technology Upgrade manager that would account for his workplace bullying. The following section will take you behind his interpersonal behavior and focus on what was going through his mind that, to him at least, not only justifies his behavior but makes it desirable.

Character Cameo Three: Driven to Aggressive Management

At the start of the action a raw and inexperienced but ambitious and driven technology manager is given a challenging and responsible position. He has had some management development but not that much. His driven and rugged style, combined with his lack of empathy and lack of coaching skills, mean that he only has one way of managing his team when he perceives that things are going wrong: he puts them under pressure. He justifies this approach by telling himself that

- Dealing with them in this way will toughen up his team for their dealings with the front office.
- He respects it in his managers.
- Finance is a tough business for tough people.
- Putting his team under pressure will separate the wheat from the chaff.

The manager has little or no understanding of either himself or anyone else, and doesn't respect value systems which differ from his own. He is extremely task-focused and driven, and expects his team to handle things in ways he approves of. When they don't, his first reaction is to mistrust their competence: not his own style of managing them or the validity of some of the complaints made against them by the front office.

In his new role he finds himself managing some team members who are less forthcoming and less robust than he'd like them to be and this frustrates him. He doesn't know how to flex his management style to bring the best out of them and resorts to bullying behavior instead, having decided – albeit subconsciously – that this is the only way to turn around these particular staff who he thinks of as under-performing. Actually, on the quiet, he despises some of his more guarded and cautious colleagues and values the opportunity to tell them so, no matter how he dresses it up as feedback on their performance.

The Technology Upgrade manager is also terrified of failure. Worse still, he has come to believe that any style different from his own is bound to fail in the tough world of finance. He simultaneously over-values his own way of doing things and under-values all other ways of doing things. As soon as a front office client makes a complaint about one of his team it is as if that client has pressed a red button in the manager's psyche. Instead of supporting his team member, helping him develop and managing his client's expectations, he sees red and goes on the attack.

He starts to use a highly driven and pressurizing management style with his more low-key team members, a management style which is punitive and destructive. His approach is predicated on the assumption that his team members are under-performing and that it is their responsibility to prove to him that they can cut the mustard. This combination of a highly mistrusting and highly pressurizing management style undermines his staff, and some of his behavior constitutes workplace bullying. One of the people he is most unpleasant to, someone who is both reticent and quiet, has an excellent reputation in the department. The manager seeks to overpower him with aggressive, unjustified negative feedback on his personality. His feedback ignores all the strengths of his team member's performance and deliberately overlooks all his well-documented qualities: qualities like thoroughness, attention to detail and sensible caution, all of which contribute to him being an effective technologist. The manager attacks him personally, characterizing him as a 'chicken with the front office', telling him to 'toughen up' and informing him that he'll be all over him 'like a rash' from that point on.

This combination of castigatory comments about his personality, and no respect for any of his positive qualities or past achievements, crush the team member and result in him wanting to leave the team. The manager then plays his trump card and refuses the technologist the right to leave the team, effectively keeping him on site so that he can continue to subject him to confusing and penalizing bullying behavior. The team member feels trapped and starts to make mistakes, mistakes which are highlighted by both his manager and his clients, providing more ammunition for the manager to use against him in subsequent conversations between them. Unless the technologist can find a way to handle his boss's increasingly unreasonable and bullying style of dealing with him, he will find that his psychological and emotional well-being are in jeopardy.

***

In the instance above an ambitious young man is placed in a position of significant organizational responsibility without having the management skills, self-awareness or maturity to handle his challenging role effectively. His personal beliefs around what kinds of behavior do and do not constitute effective service to front office clients results in him using a highly pressurizing management style with all his team; and cause him to instigate a campaign of workplace bullying against one team member whose personal style doesn't fit the bill, at least as far as he is concerned. He has no real justification for using these tactics against a member of his workforce who has an excellent track record. Rather these behaviors are evidences of his own misguided personal philosophy, poorly developed people-handling skills and vindictive character toward his meeker colleague.

KEY CAUSES OF WORKPLACE BULLYING

What conclusions can we draw from the three instances of workplace bullying described earlier? In each case the colleague who starts to use bullying behavior at work has a personal set of reasons for doing so. These include that they:

- Fear failing publicly at work and fear the subsequent humiliation that failure will bring them; so they look for someone to scapegoat in a misguided attempt to feel better about themselves.
- Are under-performing but rather than address their own performance issues they deflect them onto a colleague and tell them that their performance is substandard when it isn't.
- Fear, quite irrationally, that their role may become threatened by a younger colleague and so bully that person in an attempt to undermine them professionally and damage their reputation with other colleagues.
- Feel jealousy or envy toward a younger colleague because of their personal qualities, or because of their rapid progress at work, and bully that colleague in an attempt to eliminate them from the workplace.

- Use their personal style preferences as a justification to attack and humiliate less aggressive colleagues who they secretly feel contempt for.
- Like throwing their weight around and puff themselves up on the bogus sense of power and competency that these tactics engender in them.

However, each of these rationales is no more than a smoke screen. None of these 'reasons' justifies the use of bullying behavior and in some cases the use of these tactics could actually hasten the personal failure that the bully so fears and seeks to avoid. In almost every case a person who uses bullying behavior is guilty of:

- Failing to develop the emotional maturity, interpersonal skills and intrapersonal self-awareness they need to handle their workplace responsibilities and work effectively with their colleagues.
- Using their time and energy to undermine and injure their colleagues instead of addressing the work issues and responsibilities that fall to them.
- Avoiding responsibility for developing the skills and competencies they need to succeed in their roles.
- Taking punitive action against effective colleagues when it is they who are under-performing.
- Taking action to leave the colleagues they bully feeling incompetent when it is they whose competence is in question.
- Scapegoating and blaming innocent colleagues in a misguided attempt to feel better about themselves.
- Generating numerous justifications, obfuscations and excuses to substantiate their use of behavior which is always reprehensible, sometimes illegal and, in most cases, likely to do serious psychological and emotional damage to the people they subject to it.

EUPHEMISMS AND EXCUSES FOR BULLYING BEHAVIOR

One of the reasons that workplace bullying is so prevalent is that it is often not seen for what it is by those who witness it, observe it or are responsible for managing the person using bullying behavior. Or, sadly, when the behavior is seen for what it is, it is overlooked and the person using bullying behavior is enabled to continue to do so. Let's take a look at some of the excuses and euphemisms which are used to justify not confronting bullying behavior:

- Consider the senior manager who witnesses or hears about the robust and aggressive tactics that one of his managers uses with a particular team member, and who decides that the way to handle this situation is to provide the person subject to the bullying with coaching to help them stand up to the bully. The senior manager thereby avoids having to do the tricky thing of confronting the bullying manager who works for him, and can comfort himself with the knowledge that he has done something to help the person subject to bullying. But, the message he has actually given to his workforce is that if anyone in the organization uses bullying behavior they will get away with it: the senior manager will place the onus for handling that behavior with the person subject to it and not confront the bully at all.
- Consider the manager who observes one of her team using bullying behavior with another member of her team. She doesn't want to get involved either, lacking the resolve and know-how to do so. So she turns a blind eye and tells herself that only weak people get bullied and that they need to learn to stand on their own two feet.
- Consider the manager who recognizes that several members of his chain of command routinely bully their team members. She talks to them about it. They tell her, variously, that 'these things happen sometimes, don't they?', that 'it's the best way to turn around under-performers' and that 'it was just an off-day'. She realizes that her bullying managers are not going to change their behavior easily and, rather than make the emotional investment needed to bring about those behavior changes, she does nothing.
- Consider the HR adviser who recognizes that one of the people in her client group is using bullying behavior. She tells her manager what she has observed. Her manager tells her that she must have misinterpreted what she saw. When the HR advisor replies that she is absolutely sure she has witnessed several instances of bullying behavior by the same person, her manager tells her that 'people respect strong management' and that her team member is 'getting it out of all proportion'.

There are numerous excuses made for workplace bullies by those who work alongside them or manage them. There are also numerous euphemisms used to reduce workplace bullying to something more acceptable. The fact remains that when workplace bullying is tolerated it sends out the message to the workforce that, should any of them be subject to workplace bullying, they will likely be left to manage the situation themselves.

SUMMARY AND NEXT CHAPTER

This chapter has examined why people use bullying behavior at work. It has focused on identifying the key causes of workplace bullying and incorporated three character cameos to:

- Examine the disposition of workplace bullies.
- Identify a range of intrapersonal factors which can underlie the use of bullying behavior in the workplace.
- Highlight a range of factors that people who use bullying behavior cite to justify their actions.
- Outline some of the euphemisms and excuses that are used by managers who witness bullying behavior in their workplaces and don't act to stop it.

The next chapter will focus on people who are subject to workplace bullying, and those who observe it being used against their colleagues and worry that they might also be targeted by a workplace bully.

CHAPTER 3

Sowing The Seeds for Bullying
The First Interactions Between
a Bully and Their Target

In this chapter we'll be considering your early encounters with bullying behavior. We'll be examining these encounters from the perspective of those of you who have been bullied, are being bullied or fear that you might be bullied in the future. We will explore how a bully might interact with you in the opening stages of a campaign of bullying. We'll highlight the red flags that bullies inevitably put up as they do this; red flags that, if you don't know what to look out for, you might inadvertently misinterpret, ignore or play down when you really need to heed their warnings.

The aim of this chapter is to highlight some of the tactics that bullies use early on in a campaign of bullying, especially when you haven't worked with them before and so don't know their character. However, we'll also highlight how people whose character is known to you can alter their pattern of behavior and start to use bullying behavior, even with people who they have apparently liked and worked well with. The chapter will identify some of the key dynamics that workplace bullies want to set in motion in the early stages of their bullying. It will also set the scene for some of the interpersonal strategies that we'll be examining in subsequent chapters. These will help you send a message to a bully, who you fear might be targeting you, that their bullying behavior will not prevail against you in the long run and will interrupt the bullying dynamic they are attempting to set in play in the relationship.

WHO GETS BULLIED AT WORK?

Before we go any further let me say a bit about who gets bullied at work. I think it is misleading to say that only passive or unassertive people get bullied at work. It is undoubtedly true that those of you who have a hard time responding assertively in the workplace may be more vulnerable should you come up against a workplace bully; and in many cases people who use unassertive behavior can be the preferred targets of workplace

bullies. But it is also true to say that those of you who are confident and
self-assured could also become subject to workplace bullying, and very
often this group of people can be as angry and confused as a more timid
or meek person by the bullying aggression they receive.

So let's now look in more detail at:

- The choice of who to target which is made by the bully.
- The situation in which the bully starts to test the waters to see if
  they'll get away with bullying behavior in the longer term.

It is this combination of factors which is the subject of this chapter.
This dual approach avoids the risk of placing culpability for being
bullied with the target of bullying and leaves it instead with the bully.
It makes a statement that the responsibility for workplace bullying
rests solely with the workplace bully – not the person they target – and
that a range of individual factors influences each bully's decision about
who to target. One of factors is often the character traits of the person
they eventually decide to bully – but another is the circumstance in
which they first meet their potential target.

THREE DIFFERENT SITUATIONS IN WHICH
BULLIES ENCOUNTER POTENTIAL TARGETS

In this chapter we'll make a distinction between three different situations in which a bully and their potential target encounter one another.
These are as follows:

- A job interview where the bully is one of the interviewers and the
  person they subsequently target is a candidate for the job. In this
  case the bully is meeting the candidate for the first time at the interview and can have no firsthand prior knowledge of their interpersonal style or character traits.
- A colleague moving from one department or location to another
  within the same organisation. In this case the colleague who becomes
  a target of workplace bullying has met his future bullying colleague at
  different meetings and events over the years, and formed a superficial
  view about their character, but has not worked closely with them.
- A functioning – or even cordial – workplace relationship which,
  after a period of time, becomes one characterized by one of the two
  colleagues bullying the other. In this case the two colleagues' characters
  are well known to one another and they could even be friends.

These distinctions are important because each relationship starts
on a different footing. In this chapter we will examine all three

situations and highlight ways in which a bully sows the seeds that provide clues about their future bullying conduct. We will do this through the use of three examples. Let's start by taking a look at two examples in which bullying begins during a job interview.

EXAMPLES ONE AND TWO: SETTING UP BULLYING DURING A JOB INTERVIEW

When you attend a job interview you are likely to be nervous. You must be, at the very least, interested in the role or you wouldn't have gone for the interview. You mostly likely want to make a good impression and want to be seen as responsive, responsible and likely to succeed in the role. You want to sell yourself. The focus is on you and your suitability for the job and you want to put yourself across in the best possible light. The problem is that, as you are so keen to make a good impression, you might not be listening as hard as you could be for clues about the conduct, character and values of the people interviewing you – people already employed by the organization who will provide useful benchmarks of its cultural character. What if one of these people is a bully? What should you be on the look out for? Let's consider an example:

Example One: Joining the Firm

An assertive, pert and confident young woman is made redundant by the specialist building trade supplier which employed her for ten years. The young woman was successful and effective in her role and respected by her hard-to-please clients. Her role took her on site visits to large building sites across the UK, journeys she usually made single-handedly in her company car.

Her client base was entirely made up of building contractors and site managers. Used to holding her own in a male dominated working environment, the young woman was initially upset at being made redundant. However, she decided to make the best of it, take the opportunity to retrain as an IT specialist and work on contract to global businesses, hopefully securing a role overseas. She gained the qualifications she needed and started to work, through a specialist agency, on a series of six-month contracts in the UK. She quickly became attached to working this way, and enjoyed the fact that after six months she'd have a change of scene, company, colleagues and location to look forward to. She also appreciated the fact that she could earn much more money working on a contract basis than she could earn as a full-time employee. She was relieved not to have to take up a permanent position with one employer again and determined to continue to work this way in future.

On completing her third six-month contract, and with money in the bank, she was sent by her agency to attend an interview with a large firm based in the London. The interview panel consisted of three people and the interview went well. At the end of the interview she was offered a role working in the IT Group in the firm's New York office. Delighted, she asked who she'd be reporting to and was surprised to learn that the person who'd spoken most at the interview would be her boss. He hadn't mentioned this fact before. The role, its location and the experience with which it would provide her seemed great and her instincts were to take the role but, just to be sure, she asked him what provisions the contract would make should she wish to terminate it before the six-month term was up.

The interviewer stiffened slightly and, without blinking, told her that the role was full-time. The young woman was taken aback and said that she was expecting and would prefer a six-month contract, a rolling contract if it suited him better. He replied, again without breaking step, that it was a permanent, full-time role. He tapped his forefinger slowly and deliberately on the tabletop as he said this, one tap for each word. The young woman repeated that an initial six-month period would give them both a chance to see if they suited one another. The interviewer snapped back that it was a permanent, full-time role and that if she wasn't interested in it he'd offer it to someone else who he'd interviewed that morning. The young woman accepted the role and so accepted the consequences of working for a man who had already proved himself to be underhand and coercive. Six months later she made a complaint against him for workplace bullying.

Joining the Firm: Analyzing the Dynamics

Let's now take a closer look at what happened at this interview. In particular, let's focus on the red flags that, had she been alert to them, could have given the young woman pause for thought about working for this manager, and might have prevented her from subsequently being subject to workplace bullying.

Firstly, from the very beginning, the way the interview is conducted raises questions about the lack of transparency of the interviewers. No one tells her that the role will involve reporting to one of the three people on the panel. The omission of this important piece of information is not likely to have been due to an oversight. It is much more likely to be a deliberate strategy employed by the manager involved which gives him the opportunity to surprise the candidates at some stage during the interview and see how they react: both to the news of him being their potential new manager and to the strategy of him initially withholding this piece of information and then tactically introducing it.

The young woman doesn't express surprise at either instance. She may *feel* it but, for some reason, she isn't able to convey surprise either verbally or nonverbally. She doesn't put the ball back into his court and ask why he hadn't volunteered the information sooner. She doesn't say 'that's a surprise' or 'that wasn't clear to me until just now'. Instead, she carries on as normal and continues with the interview. She fails to pick up on the significance of what has just happened. She doesn't realize that her potential new manager withholds information as a tactic to give him the upper hand and is therefore a skilled manipulator of information and workplace meetings. This does not, of course, make him a potential bully but it is a red flag that would have helped her notice.

Secondly, immediately following the revelation about who her potential new manager will be, the young woman asks about an issue close to her heart. She enquires, quite assertively, about the nature of the early termination clause of the contract and is again surprised to find out that the position is actually full-time and not a six-month contract as she had been led to believe. Her agency deals only in contract work so, once more, here is a significant red flag. It looks as if the manager has deliberately gone through a contract-based recruitment agency but is actually offering a full-time role. Why would he do this? It's about power: he does this to wrong-foot the employee and take advantage. He knows that someone who prefers to work on contract doesn't want to make a commitment to one employer, but would prefer the flexibility and room for maneuver afforded by a six-month contract. By denying her this freedom, he will take the upper hand in the relationship. The young woman would have been well within her rights at this point in the conversation to say to the interviewer that she only works on contract. She could have asked him why he approached a contract agency with a full-time position. But she doesn't. Instead of putting him on the spot, she does something just as admirable, but not as effective. She asserts herself and asks him for what she needs: that they work together on a six-month contract to see how they suit each other. He counters with an ultimatum: accept the offer or someone else he has already interviewed will be hired instead. This behavior constitutes a third red flag. Again, the young woman doesn't read the situation for what it really is. He may or may not have interviewed this other person that morning. That isn't the point. The point is that he wants her to think he has. He wants to hire her on his terms only and isn't open to negotiating on any points at all, even ones that clearly matter to her.

She wants the job but feels cornered. Rather than walk away from a job in New York and the new challenge it represents, she accepts the role working for this devious manager and on terms that suit him and not her. She has trapped herself and handed her power to him. Not that any of this means that she could have predicted that he'd turn out to be a workplace bully. Nor does it absolve him from responsibility for subsequently bullying her. But she has had the benefit of three clear red flags to warn her of his passive aggression and his inability to work collaboratively and she has ignored all of them.

She also didn't pick up on the fourth and perhaps the most telling red flag of all. Throughout the whole interview process the other two people on the panel remained silent, going along passively with the games and tactics being employed by the more senior manager. They don't object at any stage. They don't object to his underhand or passive-aggressive behavior. They remain silent and complicit. What does this tell us?

It tells us that the kind of behavior exhibited by the manager during the interview is likely to be consistent with behavior they have observed him using on other occasions. It tells us that they don't like to cross him and that they remain silent when he uses this behavior. Maybe they don't feel that it is their place to confront him; maybe they know how he reacts when people do confront him. It tells us that this is likely to be symptomatic of the kind of behavior which he knows he can get away with and so uses when it suits him. He chooses to do things this way when he thinks that no one will object, and this interview is one such occasion. It tells us that he feels confident enough to use manipulative and passive-aggressive behavior during the interview, safe in the knowledge that neither of his colleagues is likely to pick him up on it. And, if he can get away with this kind of behavior at a recruitment interview, it is likely that he will be able to get away with it on a day-to-day basis throughout the department over which he has influence. It is a fourth red flag – and a very significant indicator of the type of management style that this manager will use with the young woman once they are working together full-time.

Joining the Firm: Conclusions

So what conclusions can we draw from this example? Firstly, we can say that the young woman was unwise to accept the job; but we can also understand why she did accept it. She'd move to New York, gain good experience and work for a global firm. But she also put herself in a parlous position, working for an unpleasant and potentially nasty manager, and only time would tell just how precarious her position would turn out to be.

Secondly, none of the four red flags described above prove conclusively that this manager will turn out to be a workplace bully. Certainly they point to the fact that he is capable of using calculating and controlling behavior and will probably be a nightmare to work for. But while these red flags do not constitute positive proof that he will start a systematic campaign of workplace bullying against the young woman, they do suggest that he could be capable of such a thing.

Thirdly, the young woman accepted the job with her eyes wide open. She had money in the bank and did not have to take the job: she could have gone back to the agency and asked for another placement. Sadly, she elected to work for a man who had made his intentions clear from the off; and with whom a pattern of using passive-aggressive and manipulative behavior with her had already been set at the interview.

* * *

In the above example a young woman turns up for an interview and meets an interviewer she has not met before. She:

- Is not at all prepared for his behavioral tactics at the interview.
- Doesn't really see them for what they are.
- Is not under any pressing financial pressure to take the job.
- Decides to accept the job, believing it to be too good an opportunity to miss.
- Lives to regret her decision.

This is an example of a bullying dynamic being set in place during an interview for a role that the young woman very much wants to secure – so much so that she overlooks the obvious red flags that are inherent in the situation.

Let's now move on to examine a second instance of a bullying dynamic being set in place. This time the dynamic is different, involving as it does a colleague moving from one location to another within the same employer. Furthermore, the teacher at the heart of this example feels that he very much needs the job he is applying for as he is the only income generator in his household. Let's see what happens:

Example Two: Collusive Bullying

A biology teacher is asked to take redeployment and is offered several potential positions in his geographic region. However, only one of these posts is in the inner city in which he currently lives and works. He knows this school by reputation and has met its Head of Biology at various interschool events over the years. They have spoken once but he only has a sketchy idea of her character, having formed the view that she was both charming and outgoing from observing her at interschool events. The new school is a fair distance from his home but close enough that he wouldn't have to ask his family to move house should he accept a job there. As part of the redeployment process he is asked to meet a selection of his potential new colleagues. He accepts the invitation to attend the meeting which he is told will be with the Deputy Head, the Head of Biology and up to two other existing members of staff.

When the Biology teacher arrives at the school, he is shown into the meeting room. The four members of staff are already seated in a row on one side of a desk and the Biology teacher sits down in the vacant seat on the other side of the desk. The meeting goes well enough although only one of the four people speaks with him. This person is the Head of Biology who reports directly to the Deputy Head, who is also present. The Biology teacher is asked to return for a second meeting and he is asked if he wants the job. On this occasion he meets only the Head of Biology and the Deputy Head. This meeting takes place in the Deputy Head's office.

Once more the Head of Biology is the person who does all the talking. Up until this point the Head of Biology has been efficient if cold, behavior which puzzles the teacher as it is at odds with the more warm behavior he has encountered in her at interschool events. However, her manner changes once she is in the Deputy Head's office. She is brusque, offhand and quite openly makes two derogatory comments about specific named members of staff. She also suggests that many of the children at the school are 'illiterate and un-teachable'. At one point she stands up and, looming over the seated Biology teacher with her hands on her hips, moves to stand directly in front of him. In full view of the silent Deputy Head she says to the Biology teacher 'I am your boss. Is that clearly understood?' The Biology teacher is lost for words and merely says 'sure'.

He starts work the following Monday and has a two-hour meeting with the Head of Biology in a meeting room as part of his induction process. The Head of Biology uses the meeting to make offensive and rude comments about a number of her colleagues including the School Head who she refers to as a 'useless idiot'. At the end of the meeting she leans across the table toward her new colleague and says in a menacing tone 'the first time you cross me will be the last time you do so'.

Over the next 18 months the teacher is subject to constant workplace bullying by the Head of Biology. He isn't the only one. The whole

Biology department is scared of her and during the first six months that the teacher works there, one of his departmental colleagues resigns midterm and another is signed off work with stress.

Collusive Bullying: Analyzing the Dynamics

What happened during the redeployment process that, had the biology teacher been alert to the danger signs, could have prevented him from accepting a role which resulted in him subsequently becoming subject to workplace bullying?

Firstly, although the first meeting seems orderly enough, it is odd that the teacher is seated opposite everyone else and that only one of the four other people at the meeting speaks with him. There could be many reasons for this, and without further evidence, it will be difficult for the teacher to make an accurate interpretation about it. A sensible thing for him to do would be to make a mental note that this seems unusual and look for further opportunities during the redeployment process to test the waters and find out why the meeting was conducted in this fashion.

Secondly, the rubber hits the road during his second visit to the school. Now the truth about the conduct of the Head of Biology and her collusion with the Deputy Head comes out. The Head of Biology is rude about two of her colleagues and about the children who attend the school in front of the Deputy Head. She is quite openly derogatory about these people safe in the knowledge that the Deputy Head is her ally and coconspirator, and either shares her views or doesn't object to her making these kinds of remarks out loud. What does this tell us? It tells us that the Head of Biology and the Deputy Head work together to enable a culture in which belittling and disparaging comments are made about colleagues who are not in the room at the time the comments are made. It also tells us that one of the two most influential people in the school enables this activity in the other. It raises a question mark about the conduct of the Head of the School too: does that person also collude or are they oblivious to what is going on?

Thirdly, the Head of Biology turns on the new teacher and, in no uncertain terms, tells him that he is to regard her as his boss and that she expects his utter compliance with her will. She does this brazenly and boldly in front of the Deputy Head who sits in silent endorsement of her behavior. If he had doubts before, the teacher can now be in no doubt whatsoever that these two people actively collude with one another in creating a culture whereby the Head of Biology bullies people in the department and does so on the understanding that the Deputy Head will not disapprove of her conduct. At this point the teacher needs to recognize the red flags for what they are and, at least, ask for time to consider the job offer. But he doesn't. Instead he avoids the confrontation he needs to have and, lost for words, gives verbal assent to his bullying boss's tactics with the single word reply 'sure'. He then goes on to accept a job working for a departmental head who wants to bully him and a Deputy Head who is ok with this approach.

Collusive Bullying: Conclusions

So what conclusions can we draw from this example? Firstly, we can again sympathize with the pressures on the teacher that predispose him to take the job at the school. He needs a new job and is being offered one in the same city where he lives: he would be employed as a Biology teacher which is his chosen profession; his family wouldn't have to move house; his commute would be reasonable. But joining the new school proves to be a disastrous move for him and one that he cannot easily undo.

Secondly, the silence of three of the people at the first meeting becomes more understandable as does the odd seating arrangements at that meeting. It's all about power and fear. The seats are arranged to make it feel, from the Biology teacher's point of view, like an interview not a meeting with potential new colleagues. Two of the interview panel members are too scared to speak in front of the Deputy Head and the Head of Biology. They keep quiet because it is safer for them to do that than to stick their necks out and risk contributing verbally. The Deputy Head is silent because she lets the Head of Biology speak for her instead. The Biology teacher could not have understood the full implications of this conduct when he first met his potential new colleagues, but he could have asked careful questions about the meeting or more general questions about the culture of the school on his second visit.

Thirdly, we can conclude that, on being asked if he wants the job in the Deputy Head's office, the teacher needs to consider saying no. At that meeting the Head of Biology openly uses bullying behavior with him in front of her silent senior colleague. It is a clear warning to the teacher that the Head of Biology is motivated, at least partly, by wanting power and that the fear tactics she uses to get it are fully condoned by the Deputy Head. This is a huge warning and is given to him before he formally accepts the position. When the Biology teacher doesn't heed that warning he sets himself up for a sustained experience of workplace bullying, one that could have been avoided had he stepped back from the situation and assessed his other options.

Fourthly, we can form some conclusions about the behavior and character of the Head of Biology. At interschool events she is both outgoing and bubbly but, on her home turf, she is by turns cool and distant, and then bossy and aggressive as she judges fit. What could account for this behavior change? The Head of Biology adopts a charming façade when attending interschool events. She does this to throw those outside her school off the scent and to create the impression that she is a socially adept, happy and warm person. Inside her sphere of influence, at her own school, she is punishing, bullying and uses fear to control her colleagues. Her charming persona serves her well: it creates a false impression for the people who don't work at the school, one that is convincing enough that many will not look behind the façade or enquire what might be going on behind it. Some may even be fooled enough that, should someone whisper a complaint about her to them, they'd be disinclined to believe it. It also means that her colleagues at the school are perpetually on the back foot, not knowing whether they will be dealing with her outgoing and bubbly, cool and remote or dominating and intimidating persona.

Lastly, we can conclude that the Head of Biology reserves her most castigating behavior for one of the two situations only. She is her most bullying and dominating self either when in the company of her ally, the Deputy Head; or when she is alone with the person she wishes to bully. When in the Deputy Head's office she is on safe ground and so lays all her cards on the table when she tells the Biology teacher: 'I am your boss. Is that clearly understood?' Alone in a meeting room with the Biology teacher she takes the opportunity to say to him 'the first time you cross me will be the last time you do so'. She is likely to be judicious about when she makes statements like these and will pick her opportunities carefully.

* * *

In the above example a teacher is being redeployed and arrives at a prospective new school to meet a selection of his new colleagues. He:

- Needs a new job and, preferably, one close enough to his new home so that he doesn't have to ask his family to move house.
- Has had some dealings with the Head of Biology from afar, but has not met any of the other staff at the school before.
- Doesn't expect the kind of treatment he experiences during his first and second visits to the school.
- Feels under pressure to take the post but, nevertheless, does have other redeployment choices that he could explore.

- Fails to examine these other options and subsequently deeply regrets his decision to turn a blind eye to the bullying behavior he is subject to during the redeployment process.

This is an example of a bullying dynamic being set in place during a redeployment process which gives a Biology teacher the chance of an immediate transfer to a new school. The redeployment process is conducted ruthlessly by the two people in charge of it at the new school. The Biology teacher fails to heed the warnings he is given throughout the process and, sadly, accepts a role in a department and school in which bullying is rife.

Let's now move on to examine a third instance of a bullying dynamic being set in place. This time the dynamic is very different, focusing as it does on a long-standing and effective colleague relationship that becomes one characterized by bullying. Let's see what happens:

Example Three: Change of Heart

The technology department of a large engineering firm is staffed by 15 conscientious and hardworking people, many of whom are friends and have worked side by side for years. They go for lunch together, have socialized in the evenings with their families and seem to be, on the face of it, effective colleagues and good mates. One of the two longest serving members of staff is promoted to run the department and his close colleague is the first to congratulate him.

Two days into his new role, the manager who is now in charge of the department asks his close colleague to attend a meeting with him in his office. He immediately notes that the temperature between the two men has lowered. Rather than be his usual open self, his colleague appears disagreeable and unpleasant. The new manager asks him if he is all right. His colleague doesn't answer the question but instead opens his notebook and asks 'what is this meeting about?' Over a few days he becomes increasingly difficult to deal with and eventually walks past his boss in the corridor without acknowledging his presence at all.

Over the next two months his former close colleague becomes the focus of a number of complaints from his office coworkers. He is difficult to deal with, late for meetings, rude to his peers, fails to meet deadlines for important pieces of joint work and then, on a Friday afternoon, he steps over the line. He calls one of his more reticent peers over to his desk and tells him that he has been through his computer and his paper files and he is not satisfied that they are in order. He tells his peer that he is not keeping up-to-date with his work and is letting his standards slip. Then he produces a file of papers from his briefcase and tells his peer that he has been monitoring his e-mails. He opens the file revealing a half-inch thick wad of A4 paper, each piece of which is a single e-mail sent by his colleague during the course of his work. His colleague is numbed. He says he is shocked and that he had no idea his work had been under review. He assumes, wrongly, that his work has been monitored with the say-so of his boss and cannot account for why this should be the case. Unable to speak for the shock of it, his mind whirls, he feels confused and physically sick.

Change of Heart: Analyzing the Dynamics

What happened in this scenario? One of two close friends is promoted above the other. Rather than deal with his sense of rejection and disappointment at being overlooked for the more senior role, and the awkwardness of now having to report to his friend, the second colleague lets his behavior around the office degenerate. He starts by being cold with his boss, difficult and awkward to his coworkers and, over a period of two months, misses deadlines and is rude to peers. Then he begins a campaign of bullying against one of his peers. He picks a particularly quiet and conscientious member of staff, someone with whom he has socialized, and someone who would not suspect him capable of the underhand and devious tactics he uses against him. He starts to secretly monitor his peer's e-mails and work output. When he eventually confronts this colleague with the 'evidence' against him, his peer is devastated that his work might be below par and that he has been the subject of a review carried out without his knowledge.

This is a particularly unpleasant incident of bullying to examine for several reasons:

■ Firstly, it involves one work friend turning on another out of the blue – at least as far as the bullied peer is concerned.
■ Secondly, there are so few red flags that the bullying is about to start. The most obvious signals are the general deterioration in the office conduct of the overlooked colleague. But he treats everyone in the office like this – not just the person he bullies – and deteriorating conduct isn't a predeterminant of a campaign of bullying. Nor need it be something that his colleagues will necessarily connect with him being overlooked for promotion. They might see it this way, or they might not: it would depend on a number of factors, for example how emotionally literate they are. Furthermore, the colleague who is eventually singled out for bullying is not treated any worse by the

bullying peer than anyone else – at least not until he is presented with the 'evidence' of his under-performance.

- Thirdly, the bullying colleague selects a conscientious and reserved coworker to bully: someone whose work is close to his heart, who cares deeply about the quality of his work and who is unlikely to have the interpersonal know-how to fight back.

In fact his peer is so defeated by the passive-aggressive tactics used against him that he wrongly assumes that the departmental manager must have sanctioned them. It never occurs to him that the colleague presenting him with a file of his e-mails has taken it upon himself to monitor him in this way. It doesn't occur to him that his peer's sole motivation for doing this is to find a scapegoat upon whom to take out his bitterness and anger at being overlooked for promotion, and that he has picked someone who is both competent at his job and interpersonally less able than him because he sees him firstly, as some-one who is effective at his job and whom he wishes to undermine; and secondly, as a soft target for ongoing bullying.

So, what can we learn from this situation? The way forward for the bullied colleague is to focus on the facts. These include that he:

- And his work has been under review without his knowledge.
- Hadn't been told that his work might be substandard before the monitoring started.
- Needs to understand what is perceived to be wrong with his work and who authorized that it be monitored.

His bullying colleague is actually taking quite a risk. He hopes that his crushed colleague will simply believe what he says – that his work standards have slipped – and that his long-standing relationship with the new departmental manager will mean that he gets away with it, either because the bullied colleague will assume that the review has been sanc-tioned by the boss, or because he will be so floored by it that he won't think to check out the facts. The bullying colleague's hope is that his peer will not be able to face going to see his boss for fear that his boss will say 'yes, your work is below par, and yes, I did order your work to be monitored'. However, that is exactly what the bullied peer needs to do: go and see his boss and trust that the facts will speak for themselves. The facts are that:

- He has an excellent track record with the department.
- His standards have not slipped as far as he knows.

- He hasn't received any negative feedback about his performance up until this point.
- But: his e-mails have been monitored all the same.
- He has been told by his peer that his work is below par, although he has been given no details of what is wrong with it.
- He does not understand the rationale for his e-mails and work being monitored; nor does he know what is problematic about his performance.

With these facts his boss will likely conclude that something is amiss and, having investigated, will realize that:

- His erstwhile close friend has grossly exceeded his authority and given misleading and disingenuous feedback to a conscientious and effective member of the team
- It is his responsibility to sanction his former close friend and prevent him from taking such action in the future.

How he chooses to handle this situation will be an early test of his ability as a leader. He must be seen to take his former close friend in hand – and he must make it clear that there is nothing real with which to reproach his bullied peer.

Change of Heart: Conclusions

So what conclusions can we draw from this example? Firstly, we can say that to target a conscientious and competent member of staff and tell them that they are under-performing is a pernicious thing to do. Anyone who prides themselves on their work and puts a lot of themselves into it will be injured and undermined by this move. The bullying colleague does just that in a cynical attempt to leave his conscientious colleague feeling as bad as he does, although for very different reasons. It is a crude attempt at scapegoating.

Secondly, we can conclude that the bullying peer's strategy is simply about power: hit his colleague and hit him hard, and hope that he is too stunned to fight back. In truth, if the colleague can find it in himself to question what he is being told he will quickly find that there isn't anything to the 'charges' against him. The review of his work hasn't been sanctioned from above; there is nothing wrong with his performance; and the 'evidence' against him is an innocent file of his e-mails. However, if the bullied colleague assumes that there is truth in the accusation that his work is sub-standard, and starts to look inward to try and find out where he is failing, he may start a cycle of self-doubt that debilitates him. He may not feel able to check out the facts with his departmental manager, he may continue to think that his peers and senior manager think he is under-performing and he may become even more demoralized. He may also leave himself open to continued bullying from his peer. Then his work might really suffer and he may be held accountable for working below par.

Thirdly, we can conclude that the bullying peer's emotional self-awareness and self-management are very poor indeed. Rather than deal with his own anger and hurt at being overlooked for promotion, and his humiliation that his close friend is promoted above him, he is cold to his erstwhile friend and rude to everyone else in the office. He decides to scapegoat a perfectly competent peer and sets about planning an unfounded attack on a diligent but unassertive colleague: a cowardly thing to do.

SUMMARY AND NEXT CHAPTER

This chapter has been about three different situations in which bullies set about their work: with people they've never met before, with people they have some passing knowledge of and with long-standing colleagues. It has highlighted:

- A variety of red flags and warnings that bullies put up in advance of starting to bully.
- How to interpret these signals and react to them.
- The dangers of misinterpreting these red flags or of underplaying their significance.
- How to use the facts and the truth to stand your ground against an unfounded accusation that your work is substandard.

The next chapter will focus on perhaps the two key issues at the heart of the bullying relationship: the power of the bully and the choices you have in the moment you are subject to bullying behavior.

CHAPTER 4

The Bullying Dynamic
Issues of Power and Choice at The Heart of a Bullying Relationship

In this chapter we will investigate the nature of the bullying dynamic between you and the person who is bullying you. We will do this by considering two key facets of the relationship between you and your assailant: the interconnected issues of their power and your choices which lie at the heart of a bullying relationship.

This chapter will illustrate how most workplace bullies try to remove power and choice from those they target. It will highlight how locating and exercising what choices you do have in an abusive situation can protect you at the time you are being bullied – and can alter the character of the bullying dynamic evolving between you. This chapter will:

- Examine some of the methods that workplace bullies might use to try and remove power from you when they undertake a campaign of bullying against you.
- Identify some of the choices that you have in a bullying situation – even if they are limited – choices which, if judiciously employed, can preserve some or all of your power and send the message to the bully that they won't have it all their own way.

You will see that, while it isn't always easy, you do have options about how you respond to the power tactics that bullies use: choices which, when wisely executed, can help your cause in the short and the long run, and which can interrupt the bullying dynamic that the workplace bully is trying to introduce into their relationship with you.

The aim of this chapter is twofold. Firstly, it will prepare those of you who are yet to become the target of a workplace bully about the tactics that bullies might use in their campaigns. My hope is that those of you in this situation will be forewarned and forearmed: alert to the danger of mishandling a bullying behavior and therefore being vulnerable to the bully from that point onward. Secondly, for those of you already subject to workplace bullying, you will have a chance to reconsider the patterns of behavior between you and your bullying colleague. My hope is that you will be able to identify different ways in which to handle their bullying behavior and make choices which give the bully pause for thought.

The objectives of this chapter are to:

- Define the term 'bullying dynamic'.
- Make clear the role that you, the bullied person, play in the relationship between you and the person bullying you.
- Explore the nature of 'power' as it relates to workplace bullying.
- Describe the differences in their attitude to workplace power and to their colleagues' choices between a nonbullying colleague and a bullying colleague.
- Explore what it means for a workplace bully to try and 'remove power' from you.
- Explore how you can inadvertently give your power away to a bully or fail to preserve it from them.
- Clarify how to identify and exercise the choices available to you in a potentially abusive situation.
- Examine how the judicious exercise of these choices can interrupt the bullying dynamic that the bully is trying to create in their relationship with you and cause them to think again.

CREATING A BULLYING DYNAMIC

A person who has determined to bully you has to start somewhere. At some point in their relationship with you they will start to use behavior which reveals their agenda to bully. The behavior they use to denote this fact could be subtle or blatant or somewhere in between. It could happen in a one-to-one meeting with you or in a setting that includes other people as well. But whenever it happens, is when your colleague's behavior signals that, from this point onward, they will set about:

- Removing power from you and placing it with themselves.
- Limiting the choices you have about how you conduct yourself at work.
- Introducing a bullying dynamic into the relationship – one which they hope will become an established way of interacting between the two of you.

Different workplace bullies will use different tactics to achieve these three interconnected aims. But however they go about it their aim is to create a dynamic in their relationship with you which facilitates their aggressive, coercive behavior and keeps you on the defensive. In attempting to create this dynamic a workplace bully might employ a range of tactics such as:

- Introducing abusive behavior into their relationship with you to confuse and disable you.
- Seizing the initiative while you are off balance and wrong-footed.
- Using fear as a tool to secure your compliance.
- Intimidating you in front of other people to secure their silence and therefore their complicity in exchange for not being targeted – and leave you feeling that you have no allies who will actively stand with you.

Workplace bullies use tactics like these in an attempt to create a bullying dynamic in their relationship with you. But what does the term bullying dynamic actually mean? The bullying dynamic is the two-way relational street between you and the person who wants to bully you. The bullying dynamic is about:

- The aggressive, unreasonable and coercive behavior the bully uses with you.
- Your response to that behavior at the time it is happening.
- The patterns of behavior that are therefore established between you.

The bully would like their relationship with you to be conducted along lines where they use coercive force and you comply with their wishes – at least outwardly. You may silently fume at the time and inwardly resent them afterward but it's what you say and do outwardly at the time you are being bullied that maintains or interrupts the bullying dynamic.

    The bully would like to feel in charge of you and your actions and would prefer that you use compliant behavior which helps to maintain this balance. This is not to say that you, the person being bullied, are responsible for whether or not the bullying activity continues: this responsibility lies fairly and squarely with the bully themselves. But it is true to say that, even if your options are limited, you will have some choices about how to respond to bullying behavior at the time it happens – and it is also true to say that the quality of your response can alter the dynamic that the bully is trying to put into play. It is with the wise exercise of these choices that your true power lies in an abusive, bullying situation.

Let's examine the nature of the bullying dynamic by comparing the way that nonbullying colleagues and bullying colleagues handle their power and your choices at work. Consider the following two descriptions of what it's like to work alongside nonbullying colleagues and what it's like to work with bullying colleagues. You might like to compare them with your own experiences.

WORKING WITH NONBULLYING COLLEAGUES

In normal, nonbullying workplace relationships you and your colleagues will likely set out to work together constructively. You will usually listen to one another's viewpoints, discuss ideas openly and receptively, respect each other's points of view even if you don't agree with them and express differing options without coming to blows or falling out. You may disagree, quarrel and get cross with one another from time to time but, in the main, you will likely want to make joint decisions that you can all agree on – or at least that you all can live with. Equally, while your boss might decide to overrule some of your decisions or instruct you to carry out certain tasks in specific ways, their reasons for doing so are valid and not abusive or about power.

In this sense neither you nor any of your colleagues wants to prevail over anyone else. You may choose to defer to one another's greater expertise on various matters, and you may also choose to take direction from one another based on your differing roles, levels of organizational authority or energy levels at any given time. You may also find that one or other of you has strongly held and passionately voiced views on some matters and wants to influence those issues more than other issues they care less about. But, crucially, the process of working together will be largely negotiated and none of you will think that your will or views are regarded as consistently subservient or superior to anyone else's. In other words: power is not an issue between you and the process of your joint work will likely be characterized by open exploration of different opinions, freedom to choose how you approach your work, mutuality and give and take.

WORKING WITH BULLYING COLLEAGUES

However, when working alongside a workplace bully it is a wholly different ball game. *The bully makes the relationship about power: their power over you.* They use behavior which is dominating, dictatorial and intimidating. They use fear to control you and don't want their working relationship with you to be characterized by partnership or collaboration. They want to hold sway over you. They want to control your behavior and they think they are entitled to hold as much power in the relationship as they can. They want to tell you what to do, expect you to take their orders and don't mind overriding your will. They will assume the right to approach their relationship with you on these terms and will use behavior which they hope provides you with little choice but to comply. In other words they will take it upon themselves to coerce you through dint of personality into doing their will because they hope you:

- Fear the consequences of refusing to do what they want.
- Don't want to fight back.
- Won't know how to handle the situation assertively enough and so will give in to their wishes whether you want to or not.

DISREGARDING YOUR BOUNDARIES AND YOUR CHOICES

There are obvious interpersonal differences between behavior you can expect from a colleague who wants to handle their relationship with you in a normal, nonbullying way and behavior you can expect from a colleague who wants to bully you. Some of these are highlighted above and you may be able to add more based on your own experiences of workplace bullying.

But what are the key intrapersonal differences between the two approaches to working with you? The key difference is that the non-bullying colleague respects your personal boundaries and your choices and the bullying colleague does not. The bullying colleague doesn't respect the boundaries around your work or your workplace responsibilities and doesn't respect your right to choose, within the parameters of your role, how you will carry out your duties.

Some bullies don't see these boundaries at all. Others do recognize that these exist but often override, ignore and disregard some or all of them. The effect of the constant erosion of your boundaries over time can be to render you feeling powerless in the relationship and to leave you feeling treated as an object, not a person.

Consider the following example:

Example One: Blindsided

A communications manager in a retail bank head office is subject to workplace bullying by his boss. He endures this treatment alone and doesn't speak to anyone at work about the bullying he is subject to, bullying which usually happens in one-to-one meetings between him and his boss.

After two months of relentless workplace bullying the communications manager takes planned time off for a routine operation. While he is away he speaks with his colleagues in the office. After nearly two weeks off work he tells them that he will return to work on a Friday afternoon. His boss is unavailable when he tries to contact him so he asks two different colleagues to pass this information on to him.

On Friday afternoon he returns to work and is met by his furious manager who walks him into his office and closes the door behind them. His manager angrily tells him that he is late for work and that, having been off work for the best part of two weeks, the least he could have done is to get in on time on the day of his return. Without waiting for a reply he hands the communications manager a pile of paperwork, tells him 'to get on with it' and walks smartly toward the door.

There are a number of ways in which the communications manager could respond to this situation. Let's explore three of them:

- The communications manager is so shocked and floored by this abusive interview that he is lost for words. He cannot believe that his manager has just behaved in this way the minute he stepped foot into his workplace. In the time it takes him to think these thoughts his manager leaves the room closing the door behind him. The communications manager stays in the office trying to gather his thoughts and then returns to his desk with the pile of paperwork feeling dazed and confused.
- The communications manager is shocked and floored by this abusive interview and takes a few minutes to recover his composure. He lets his manager leave the room, returns to his desk, places the files on it and takes a deep breath. Then he looks around to find out where his manager is. He sees him at the far end of the open plan office, near the photocopier, and goes over to speak to him. He explains that he thinks there has been a misunderstanding between them about the timing of his return to work that day. He says that he had left two separate messages for him explaining that he would be arriving in the afternoon not the morning. He says that he would have expected at least one of the messages to have got through and can't understand why they appear not to have done.
- The communications manager is shocked at being spoken to like this but he is not at all floored by it. He is angered by the interview.

He takes the paperwork from his boss but then immediately places the files firmly on his boss's desk and turns to face him. His expression is one of serious intent and his tone when he speaks is considered. He looks his boss in the eye and, using a firm, even tone, an unwavering pace of delivery and maintaining eye contact with his boss throughout, he says that he isn't late. He informs his boss that he had already left two messages for him telling him that he would be returning to work that afternoon. He says that if his boss hadn't got either message he should still have had sufficient respect to ask him how he was feeling after surgery before saying anything else. He says that his view on what has just happened is that his boss is taking his anger out on him unjustifiably and that he prefers not to be spoken to like that again. He then says that he is comfortable agreeing the work that his boss wants him to do on a case-by-case basis so that he can discuss the work with him and they can agree on timescales for the completion of the tasks. He tells him that he is uncomfortable having work dumped on him without any discussion about suitable timescales for completing it and that he doesn't think this is a productive way for the two of them to work together. Then he is silent. His boss is stunned and for a moment doesn't know what to say. He shakes himself and says, in a strained voice, that the communications manager can look over the work and report to him on when he will be able to complete it. Then he leaves the office visibly discomforted.

Blindsided: Analyzing the Dynamics

Let's take a look at what is happening in the action described above starting with the conduct of the boss. We will focus this part of the analysis on the extent to which the boss disregards his communications manager's choices and personal boundaries by attacking him the moment he returns to work:

The Boss's Conduct: The first point to make is that the boss displays basic discourtesy for the communications manager as a person. He doesn't ask him how he is, how the operation went or how his recuperation is going. He doesn't suggest that he sit down to take the weight off his feet nor does he ask him what it feels like to be back at work after nearly two weeks off. Do these omissions constitute disregard for his personal boundaries and choices? Probably not, but they do tell the communications manager that his boss is demonstrating contempt for his welfare and that, in the absence of at least one question about how he is, is not at all interested in how he is feeling. While in and of themselves these omissions do not constitute an abuse of power, they ought to put the communications manager on his guard.

Secondly, the boss shows no respect for the communications manager as a member of his workforce. He doesn't ask him how he'd like to manage his return to work, what plans he has for the afternoon or where he'd like to start to get up to speed with what has happened during the previous two weeks. Instead, he assumes that the communications manager is slacking and launches into an attack, telling him that he is late for work and immediately handing him a pile of things to do. Do these actions constitute a disregard of his workplace boundaries and choices? Yes they do. He disregards the communications manager's choices about how and when to return to work, how to reintegrate with the workplace after his time away and what route he'd like to choose to enable him to catch up with what he's missed while being off work. Instead he uses the meeting as an opportunity to vent his anger and dump work on his colleague without providing him with an opening to speak. He then tries to leave the room. This approach certainly constitutes a clear disregard for the communications manager's workplace boundaries and choices by someone who has already demonstrated himself capable of using bullying behavior.

Thirdly, the manner of the boss's attack is calculated to provide the communications manager with no opportunity to defend himself, ask a question or, actually, say anything at all. The timing of the attack – as soon as the communications manager steps into the office after nearly two weeks on sick leave – is designed to put him onto the back foot straight away. The boss hits him while he is still finding his feet and does so quite deliberately. This strategy is designed to give the communications manager the clear message that, as far as the boss is concerned, the more vulnerable he feels the better. He hopes that the speed of his attack will surprise the communications manager and that it will be too late for him to point out that he had left two messages saying that his planned return to work will commence at the start of the afternoon. He hopes that it will be too late for him to state that he had always intended to return at this time and isn't actually late. He hopes that it will be too late for him to adjust to being back at work and find something to say which will enable him to handle the abusive interview effectively. He wants his surprise attack to blindside the communications manager so that he is unable to exercise any choices at all at the time his boss upbraids him. He hopes that the communications manager will fail to do anything to inhibit the bullying dynamic that the boss is seeking to introduce into the relationship the minute his colleague returns from his sick leave.

Having examined the conduct of the boss let's now turn our attention to the two instances of the communications manager's response. We will focus this part of the analysis on the extent to which he is able to exercise choice in an abusive situation and thereby preserve some or all of his power:

The First Instance: Sadly, being caught off guard after an operation and nearly two weeks away from the office, the communications manager doesn't predict that his boss might try and bully him as soon as he returns to work. He isn't expecting the treatment he receives and he is unable to exercise much choice at the time of the attack. His silence means that he fails to take advantage of the opportunity before him to act in a self-preserving or self-protecting way. He simply stands there in shock, holding on to the pile of paperwork as his boss leaves the office.

We can entirely sympathize with his predicament. But we can also see that his silence doesn't serve his best interests. By failing to respond to his boss's tactics he assists him in reestablishing the bullying dynamic that had existed in their relationship prior to him taking time off work. His opportunity to signal a new phase in their working relationship – a phase in which he doesn't allow himself to be bullied unopposed – has passed and his boss leaves the office believing that he can carry on bullying his colleague as and when he feels like it.

The Second Instance: The communications manager takes a few minutes to recover from the shock of being addressed so aggressively by his manager. He decides that he needs to set the record straight and, having taken a few minutes to compose himself at his desk, he goes to find his boss at the photocopier. He tells him that he had left two separate messages for him both of which told him that he would be arriving in the afternoon, not the morning. He believes that giving his boss this information will resolve the issue, which, as far as the communications manager is concerned, is a simple matter of a misunderstanding which has been blown out of proportion by his irascible boss. On the face of it this is a good start. The communications manager defends himself against the charge of being late, and points out that he cannot understand how his two messages have gone astray.

However, a closer look tells us that the communications manager hasn't really helped his cause by handling things in this way. In fact he is unlikely to have altered the bullying dynamic at all by treating this bullying incident as a simple workplace misunderstanding. Sure, he has pointed out the fact that his manager is wrong in thinking that he was late to work. But he has also failed to see the situation for what it is. He assumes that his manager hasn't actually received either message and calls the situation which has evolved between them 'a misunderstanding'. In characterizing it as a mix-up the communications manager has missed the point. In fact his boss has received both messages. He is fully aware that the communications manager plans to return to work that afternoon, not that morning, but he decides to bully him anyway on the pretext that he is late. From his point of view this is a perfect opportunity: his communications manager will arrive at work off guard, completely unprepared for an incident of workplace bullying. He will walk straight into a situation which his boss ruthlessly engineered simply so that he can attempt to reestablish the bullying dynamic between them as soon as his colleague returns to work.

In taking things at face value the communications manager doesn't address the real issues behind the behavior of his manager: his bullying behavior. If he is to alter the bullying dynamic between them then he needs to address the conduct, motives and aggression of his manager.

The Third Instance: The communications manager gathers his wits about him and responds to what his boss has just said and done. His message back to his boss, delivered in a firm voice and with level eye contact throughout, gives his boss the clear message that the communications manager reserves the right to have a say in what happens to him in the workplace. His tone and manner of delivery tell his boss that he alone is in charge of what he says and does. They convey to his boss that neither is he reacting to his boss's aggression, nor is he thrown by his boss's tactics, nor has his boss succeeded in controlling him and his behavior. Rather his manner of delivery denotes that he is choosing his response and is very much in control of what he is saying.

The manner of his rebuttal tells his boss that he will not be treated as an extension of his boss's whims, that he will not be ordered about, and that he will not allow himself to be managed or treated abusively without choosing to object to the behavior. It tells his boss that when he bullies him he will respond in a way which preserves his boundaries, his choices and therefore his personal power. He sends these messages to his boss in a way which is neither disrespectful nor aggressive, but in a way which is clear, firm and resolute. He outlines what he regards as being a more productive way for the two of them to work together: a clever thing to do as it moves the conversation back again to the real reason they are there; which is to collaborate effectively together on work for their employer.

The communications manager then falls silent while he maintains eye contact with his boss and continues to look at him with an unwavering expression on his face. He lets the silence go until his boss is forced to speak to him. He doesn't let his boss off the hook by speaking again himself. Rather he waits silently until his boss is forced to reply to what he has just said to him. He requires a response from his boss and the period of silence he lets fall retains his control of the conversation while he waits.

His boss is thrown. He has to compromise. He cannot object to what his communications manager has just said: he wasn't rude to him and he spoke about how the two of them could work better together going forward. He cannot regain the initiative through aggression: his colleague has just demonstrated that that tactic doesn't control him. His boss can no longer maintain the coercive, abusive stance he has just used and has to back down. He tells the communications manager that he can devise a schedule of when the work will be completed and report to him with it. He then attempts to save face by leaving the room.

The communications manager has redressed the balance this time. He will need to capitalize on the ground he has gained by devising the schedule and taking it to his boss. When he does so, he will need to adopt the same resolute, professional demeanor and even tempered, firm tone if he is to preserve the new status quo in the relationship. In fact he will need to adopt this approach in all his subsequent dealings with his boss.

Blindsided: Conclusions

In the above example the communications manager walks straight into an abusive situation on his return from sick leave. What conclusions can we come to about the action described above?

Firstly, we can say that the boss's actions are particularly callous, coming as they do immediately after his colleague's return to work after surgery. However, we can also say that they are very much in keeping with his previous conduct toward the communications manager who therefore could realistically have expected his boss to try and bully him on his return to work. The boss engineers a meeting with his communications manager to try and reintroduce the bullying dynamic he had established prior to his colleague's sick leave, and he does so using his usual tactic. He uses aggression to try to intimidate and control the communications manager.

Secondly, we can conclude that, no matter how appalled the communications manager is to be bullied the minute he sets foot in the workplace, he needs to gather his wits about him and respond effectively in the moment to preserve his boundaries and choices. We can conclude that should he fail to react effectively it is highly likely that the communications manager will lose power to his manager who will be well motivated to try similar tactics again in the future, safe in the knowledge that he will likely prevail again under similar circumstances.

Thirdly, we can conclude that should the communications manager react effectively at the time he is being bullied he is highly likely to pull his boss up short and turn the tables on him, perhaps, in this instance, decisively. His boss has attempted to remove power from him the minute he returns to work following surgery. For his boss to find that the communications manager is no longer an easy target for bullying behavior will be sobering for him and he will find it hard to continue in the same vein. He will be on the back foot himself and will realize that he is face-to-face with someone quite capable of defending themselves from an incident of workplace bullying, someone quite capable of putting the ball firmly back into his court. He will realize that he has been thwarted in his aim of removing power from his communications manager and reintroducing a bullying dynamic into their relationship. He may or may not try to do so again on a subsequent occasion but he will know that he will have a fight on his hands if he does try to.

Finally, we can conclude that having gained ground in the relationship, the communications manager will need to be prepared to maintain his new, assertive demeanor in all his dealings with his boss. The moment he slips back to his previous, more passive way of handling him, he can expect that his boss will try and seize the initiative again and might be tempted to try and bully him again. The communications manager will need to use all his tenacity and resolve to continue with his new approach when dealing with his boss but it will be well worth the effort. His reward will be the knowledge that he has more influence in the situation than he thought he had and that his true influence lies in his power to choose how he responds to bullying behavior.

BULLYING BOSSES

As in the above example, many workplace bullies bully their own team members. Bosses who bully have a degree of organizational authority which gives added impetus to their bullying activity and which makes them mightily intimidating figures in the workplace. Their organizational authority results in the bullying dynamic they seek to create in their relationships being all the more compelling and difficult to resist. The combination of aggressive behavior and organizational clout puts fear into the minds of the people they bully. The fear is that if you don't comply with the will of the bully then they might invoke an organizationally derived sanction against you. Sanctions they could invoke include:

- Reducing your pay.
- Demoting you.
- Canceling your holidays.
- Giving you a poor appraisal rating.
- Reducing or canceling your bonus payments.
- Making you redundant from your role.
- Giving you dull and routine work.
- Assigning you to work with people you don't enjoy working with.

However, as suggested above, even when the bully is your boss, using your personal power wisely to preserve your personal boundaries, to exercise wise choices and to handle bullying behavior *at the time it occurs* does have an impact on the bully. It does influence what the bully says and how they behave – both at the time of the incident and on subsequent occasions. In other words, it affects the dynamic between the two of you.

Consider the following three further examples:

Example Two: Unilateral Decision

A junior dentist is subject to workplace bullying by his employer, a more senior and well-respected dentist. The two men are due to attend an international dentistry conference in Prague at the end of the week. But following a particularly difficult two days, in which his boss is relentlessly critical and unpleasant, the junior dentist decides that he cannot face traveling to the conference with his employer and being subject to more abuse, this time, away from home.

He unilaterally decides to cancel his flight and hotel booking, and informs his boss that he will not be traveling. It takes a lot of courage for him to do this as he does not know how his boss will react to his decision and he fears that the bullying might escalate as a result. He will have to face the fallout from his decision on his boss's return from the trip but he has bought himself a few days respite from constant workplace bullying. In fact on his return from Prague his employer doesn't escalate the verbal bullying – he simply doesn't speak to his employee and gives him the cold shoulder. The junior dentist doesn't know how to interpret this new phase in his employer's behavior with him but decides to keep his head down and get on with his work.

Unilateral Decision: Analyzing the Dynamics

In this example the junior dentist takes a bold and self-preserving action by *unilaterally* deciding that he will not attend the Prague conference. He doesn't mention to his boss that he's having second thoughts and might not want to go. He makes his own decision and communicates that decision to his boss. This action changes the balance between them, and gives him some measure of control in an abusive situation.

His boss learns that the junior dentist can draw the line and resist him – and can do so in a nonconfrontational and self-preserving way. The bullying dynamic between them is altered and, on his return from Prague, the boss cannot find it in himself to handle his junior colleague with the same degree of verbal bullying as before the conference. Instead he ignores him which, from the junior dentist's point of view, is probably the better option of the two. It signals that his manager no longer has the upper hand and is resorting to silence instead of verbal menace as he has no other tactics to use. It may make an uncomfortable atmosphere between them but it is better than being subject to constant verbal workplace bullying.

Example Three: Reputational Risk

A university lecturer is in his lecture theatre preparing for the address he is shortly to give to his third year Geology class. The Geology lecturer has been subject to bullying behavior by the Head of Faculty since his appointment the previous year. He is assembling his lecture notes, making last minute adjustments to his slides and getting is mind in order for the ninety-minute lecture to follow.

The Head of Faculty enters the empty lecture theatre and without saying hello peremptorily tells his colleague to leave what he is doing and follow him to his office. He turns around and starts to walk toward the door simply expecting his colleague to follow him. The Geology lecturer thinks that his boss is trying to engineer a situation in which he is detained unnecessarily and so commences his lecture late, letting down his students and losing credibility with them. He is popular with his students and values his reputation with them. He decides that, whatever the real or imagined pretext for the summons to follow his boss to his office, he does not want to let his students down. He stays where he is, turns to face the Head of Faculty and tells him in a measured, firm but not impolite tone that he will not be able to follow him to his office as he has a lecture starting shortly. He informs his boss that he will come to his office after the lecture is completed. He then returns to his slides without waiting for an answer and carries on with his work.

As the students start to come into the lecture theatre the Geology lecturer looks up and is surprised to see that the Head of Faculty has not left the lecture hall at all, but is seated in the middle of the front row waiting for the class to start. The Head of Faculty sits through the lecture, making notes every now and then. He twice stands up and, in full view of the students, stretches and yawns loudly. Then, halfway through the lecture, he begins to eat a fresh apple, crunching it loudly. When the lecture is completed he leaves the room promptly without speaking to anyone.

The Geology lecturer keeps his word and, following the end of the lecture, goes to the Head of Faculty's office where he is refused admission by his boss's PA. She informs him that the Head of Faculty is busy and cannot be disturbed on trivial matters. He walks away, pleased that he didn't let his students down by starting the lecture late, and also pleased that he made it clear to the Head of Faculty that he will exercise choice rather than be ordered around. But he also realizes that his relationship with the Head of Faculty has taken a different turn and one he wasn't expecting. He does realize that, for what it's worth, the third year students witnessed the Head of Faculty's attempt to undermine him in front of them. But he is confused by his own reaction to being refused admittance to the Head of Faculty's office. Rather than take it as a snub and an indication that the stakes have been upped, he is relieved that his boss doesn't want to speak with him.

Reputational Risk: Analyzing the Dynamics

In this example the Geology lecturer draws the line at being set up by the Head of Faculty to fail his students . He decides that he will refuse his boss's order to accompany him to his office, and informs his boss of his decision to give the lecture and *then* come to meet him.

From this moment on the Head of Faculty handles the Geology lecturer differently. Firstly, he uses a greater degree of passive-aggression. He remains in the lecture theatre and, in front of all the students, he shows repeated, blatant disrespect for his colleague. He yawns, he stands up and stretches and he eats a crunchy apple. However, rather than undermine the lecturer, this approach actually shows him up – and in front of the whole of the third year. It also signals a new and different phase in his bullying campaign.

Secondly, he refuses to see the lecturer after the lecture, and asks his PA to convey to him his withering message that he hasn't got time for trivialities. The Head of Faculty may well think this action constitutes a personal snub toward the Geology lecturer and it is certainly designed to humiliate him. But the Geology lecturer doesn't see it that way and realizes that the Head of Faculty isn't used to people standing up to him and saying 'no', and can only handle that set of circumstances in one way: by childishly refusing to speak to him. He determines to stand up to his boss in that polite but firm way again and again.

Example Four: Turning the Tables

An internal consultant is designing a workshop for one of his colleagues, an investment fund manager at a financial institution in Tokyo. The internal consultant's role is to run a one-day team-building event for the investment fund manager and her team of ten people. The fund manager routinely bullies everyone in her team and, from her first meeting with the internal consultant, bullies him too. Throughout their week-long discussions about the focus and agenda for the day the fund manager bullies, humiliates and belittles the internal consultant in a sustained attempt to undermine his self-esteem and self-confidence.

The evening before the event she telephones him and tells him that she's worried the day will be 'boring'. She says that she is worried that the consultant's dull style won't cut it with her team and that, maybe, she should call the whole thing off. In the silence that follows she tells him that, in her opinion, he really isn't up to the job and hasn't managed her very well. The consultant summons up his courage and tells the fund manager that she has asked him to do a job for her, that it's too late to cancel the workshop and that she now needs to trust his judgement and let him run the day his way. The fund manager is lost for a reply and puts the phone down without saying goodbye.

The following day the consultant arrives an hour early to set up the training room. He finds that the fund manager and her entire team are already in the room, silent and bored, waiting for the workshop to begin. The fund manager is drumming her fingers on the desktop in a display of elaborate impatience. He realizes that the fund manager is continuing with her bullying tactic of trying to undermine him, this time at the start of the day, and that she has told her entire team to arrive an hour early for the workshop. The internal consultant gathers his wits about him and suggests that, as everyone has arrived an hour before the scheduled start time of the event, perhaps they could ask the venue staff to bring in some breakfast, food and drinks? His response makes it clear that the team is early rather than *him* being tardy. He also avoids two potential pitfalls: those of confronting the fund manager in front of her team which would be very unwise; and of complaining about the fact that everyone has arrived early which would set a negative and unpleasant tone at the start of the day.

Turning the Tables: Analyzing the Dynamics

In this example the internal consultant endures a week of bullying before mustering all his intrapersonal resolve and drawing the line. He tells his internal client the night before the event that she must trust him to run it effectively. This very specific word – 'trust' – goes to the heart of the matter. It unmasks her game completely and she is so at a loss for words that she puts the phone down.

She had hoped that her relentless attack on his ability and competence would cause her colleague to doubt *himself*. Instead he puts the ball right back into her court by calling a spade a spade. His choice of the word 'trust' alters the dynamic between them completely. It names her game and leaves her with nowhere to hide. It tells her that she knows exactly what she is doing and isn't fooled by her. It tells her that he can see right through her. It tells her that he can clearly perceive that the issue between them is *her* unfounded mistrust of *him* and not his supposed incompetence. She is so thrown by the truth of what he has said to her that she puts the telephone down.

The internal consultant isn't fooled by having the phone put down on him either. It could look like a rude thing to do and he might have spent the evening worrying about what to do next. He might have expended precious energy considering questions like: should he call her back? Has she already canceled the event? Actually he sees it for what it is – a signal that she is on the back foot and is flustered – and so he leaves things as they are. Unable to attack him verbally anymore the fund manager tries again, the following morning, using indirect and nonverbal means.

She assembles her entire team early in the hope of undermining the consultant at the start of the day. This ploy fails too because he is skilled at managing groups and handling the unexpected during workshops. He is easily able to turn her passive-aggression into an opportunity to enable the team to relax and have breakfast together instead. The fund manager is foiled again and the day goes well. Their working relationship is now at an end. The internal consultant no longer needs to maintain contact with this particular client – until, that is, she decides she'd like him to facilitate another team event for her. At that point, with eyes wide open, he can either take the assignment or refuse it.

THE BULLYING DYNAMIC: CONCLUSIONS

The character of the bullying dynamic in each of these four instances is altered by the actions of the person being bullied when they assert their right to make their choices their way *in the moment they are being bullied*. In doing this they send a clear message to the person bullying them. This message is that they:

- Will draw the line as and when they want to.
- Are in charge of their choices – even if the bully has lived with the illusion that they alone pull the strings.
- Can say 'no' and are prepared to take the consequences.
- Won't be intimidated into taking actions which put them in a parlous situation or compromise the quality of their work.
- Have got the measure of their assailant.

These are powerful messages to give someone who is using fear to control you. They won't like hearing them but *their behavior toward you will change* as a result of you saying these things clearly, firmly and with your head held high. Even if, at the time you draw the line, the person bullying you doesn't appear to be derailed and doesn't say anything that suggests they are uncomfortable with your assertive stance – although they might do – their subsequent behavior will change. Some bullies only need to be handled in this way once to get the message. Some of them will cease bullying you, although they might try to bully someone else instead; others will start to use more passive and more indirect means to deal with you. The trick is identifying what choices you do have and deciding where and when you want to draw the line.

IDENTIFYING YOUR CHOICES

In each of the scenarios described in this chapter there is some latitude for the person being bullied to work within, latitude which, if used effectively, will preserve some aspect of their reputation, self-confidence and/or self-esteem.

Those of you who identify with the dynamics described above will need to judge each of the bullying situations you find yourself in on a case-by-case basis. Only you can determine in which situations you want to exercise choice and in which you judge it better not to. These are fine judgement calls. My hope is that, as you become more practised at identifying and exercising your choices, you will increasingly alter any bullying dynamic developing between you and the workplace bully who is harassing you, and make it more difficult for them to prevail in the long run.

Finding and using your personal power in the moment that you are being bullied means that you preserve your energy and personal resources from being further injured or eroded by the bully. But it also requires courage and skill to handle the confrontation in a way that is assertive and self-preserving rather than in an aggressive way which will escalate the stakes even more.

SUMMARY AND NEXT CHAPTER

This chapter has examined the power dynamic at the heart of a bullying relationship. It has incorporated a series of examples to illustrate how the quality of the choices you make at the time you are being bullied can influence the ongoing dynamic between you and the person bullying you. It has explored the link between preserving your personal power, protecting your boundaries and exercising sound judgement about the behavioral choices you make to give a workplace bully the clear message that they cannot bully you unopposed.

This chapter has:

- Defined the term 'the bullying dynamic', illustrating the role that you, the bullied person, and the bully themselves play in the balance between you.
- Explored how bullies seek to remove power from those they bully.
- Focused on identifying the choices available to you at the time you are subject to workplace bullying.
- Explored a range of potential reactions to bullying tactics that could alter the bullying dynamic between you and give the workplace bully pause for thought at the time and in future.

The next chapter builds on these themes and examines further options for resisting a workplace bully. It focuses on how to read the signals that someone might be about to bully you and illustrates how to clarify your boundaries to protect yourself at the time you are being bullied.

Chapter 5

Resisting a Workplace Bully

Choosing to Assert Yourself, Managing Your Boundaries

In this chapter we will consider the issues and behaviors involved in resisting a workplace bully. We will examine how to conduct yourself should you decide that it's in your best interests to respond assertively to bullying behavior at work. We will also explore the issues you might face should you decide, for whatever reason, that you'd rather keep your head down and let the moment pass.

This chapter will identify some of the behaviors, actions and responses you could use to convey to a workplace bully that you are at least equal to their tactics and which will send them a clear message that you:

- Are not going to make it easy for them to introduce a bullying dynamic into the relationship.
- Know how to protect yourself against their intimidating behavior.

This chapter will describe the key role that the effective management of your boundaries will play in protecting yourself should you become the target of a workplace bully. You will see that it identifies a range of possible reactions you could make to bullying behavior – reactions which will cause the bully to think again as well as reactions which might encourage them to continue their campaign against you. We will explore what you could say and do should you decide to resist a workplace bully; and acknowledge that, for some of you, the experience of being bullied has left you so drained and powerless that you might decide that you do not want to resist it.

The objectives of the chapter are twofold. Firstly, it will alert those of you who fear that you might become subject to workplace bullying in the future with knowledge about the interpersonal options you have available to you should you need them. Secondly, it will enable those of you who are already subject to workplace bullying to review your handling of your relationship with the person bullying you and take steps to redress the power imbalance that has developed between you.

MANAGING YOUR BOUNDARIES: PROTECTING YOURSELF

I have written previously, and at greater length, about the nature of personal boundaries at work in Chapter 8 of *Managing Politics at Work (2009)*. For our purposes here, managing your boundaries is about giving specific, clear messages to your bullying colleague about where you draw the line and about instances in which you consider that they have stepped over that line. It is a self-preserving and self-protecting behavior to use and is absolutely vital when working with a workplace bully.

There is a close relationship between the extent to which you are able to:

- Manage your boundaries when interacting with a bully.
- Preserve and protect yourself from a bully's abusive tactics.
- Send back the message to a bully that you are going to be tough for them to deal with.
- Prevent them from successfully establishing a bullying dynamic in their relationship with you.

Consider the following example:

Example One: Starting To Bully

A large, independent department store hires a new PR manager to work alongside its marketing manager. The new PR manager is in her early 30s, and is bright, energetic and ambitious. Her new boss is in his late 50s. He has been with the company for 14 years and, on meeting him at the interview, the PR manager forms the view that he is warm, jovial and, at times, likely to drive his staff quite hard. However, she feels up to the challenge of working for him and accepts the offer of a three-year contract.

After three months of working for the department store the PR manager isn't enjoying her role very much. She has too much to do, too few people to delegate to and finds her new boss to be both unsupportive and unavailable for input. She rarely sees him and, when she does, she has difficulty getting the conversation onto the issues she wants to speak with him about. He talks at length, interrupts her regularly and keeps the meeting focused around the issues that he wants to tell her about. He doesn't listen, isn't interested in her views or opinions and doesn't give her positive feedback – only negative feedback. She feels frustrated and annoyed at working for someone who, while always pleasant and amiable, doesn't respond to her agenda and from whom she hasn't learnt very much.

On Monday morning he informs her that he has arranged to meet one of the department store's key suppliers at their office the following afternoon. The meeting is ten miles away and he wants her to accompany him to it. She is swamped with work, doesn't want to go to the meeting but feels she has little choice but to comply. That evening at six o'clock, just as she is finishing for the day, she receives a text from her boss saying: 'Hello. Re: tomorrow's meeting. Can you give me a call, thank you'. She is surprised to receive this text and can't understand why her boss doesn't just call her on her mobile as he usually does. She is tired, decides to set off home as planned and so doesn't reply straight away. She gets home, has something to eat and unwinds. She is unwilling to disturb her boss at home but wants to give him an opportunity to speak with her should he still wish to. So at eight o'clock that evening she sends him a text back saying: 'I'm free now if you want to call'.

Ten minutes later he calls her and starts by saying that he was in the shower when she rang and, as he doesn't have a phone that he can use in the shower, he wasn't able to take the call. The PR manager is shocked and disturbed by this turn of events, which she had not anticipated at all. She hadn't rung him – she'd sent him a text, and he had never spoken to her like this before. She is completely thrown, unable to find anything to say. She wonders if he has dialed the wrong number by mistake. In the silence which follows he tells her that he is unhappy with her preparation for the following day's meeting and that he expects to see a written outline of their approach to the meeting on his desk at nine o'clock the next morning.

There are a number of ways in which the PR manager could respond to this situation. Let's explore three of them:

■ She decides that her boss couldn't have meant what he just said to her. She mentally excuses him, mentally deletes everything he has said, reiterates her name and asks him what the call is about. He takes the opportunity to repeat, in a cold and angry tone, that he is not comfortable with her approach to the following day's meeting and wants a full outline of her plans for it on his desk by nine o'clock in the morning. He ends the call abruptly telling her 'it'd better be worth reading'.

- She decides that either: her boss must have dialed the wrong number or that he is losing it so, embarrassed and flustered, she ends the call hastily. She is not prepared for the fact that he calls her straight back demanding to know why she has just put the phone down on her boss in the middle of a conversation. The PR manager feels confused but asserts herself. She tells her boss that she isn't able to speak with him at that time as it is late in the evening but she will catch up with him at work in the morning. She ends the call a second time, and this time, her boss doesn't call her back.

- She thinks that her boss is way out of line and is convinced that what he has just said to her must be deliberate. *He* rang *her*. There can be no doubt that he knew who he was ringing and, on hearing her voice answering the phone and hearing her say her name on answering the call, he could have been in no doubt at all that he knew who he was speaking to. She stands tall, drawing herself up to her full height, and says in an even, firm tone that he will need to provide her with full written particulars about what he considers to be her lack of preparation for the meeting in question, preferably on the following day; and that, as the following day's meeting is his meeting not hers – and one which *he* has invited *her* to attend – she expects him to prepare for it and lead it. Then she is silent. He replies in a more relaxed tone that the meeting is important and that he'd like her to lead it. She tells him that she thinks it'd be better for the company if he leads it as he knows the background to the meeting and has set it up. She reiterates firmly that it is *his* meeting and, politely but resolutely, ends the call.

Starting to Bully: Analyzing The Dynamics

Let's take a look at what is happening in these three scenarios starting with the first one:

The First Instance: The PR manager cannot believe that her boss meant what he said. She decides to ignore his grossly improper comments to her and treat the call as a normal workplace conversation, even though it clearly isn't. The benefit, as she sees it, of handling things this way is that she can avoid a confrontation with her boss. The benefit to her of taking this line is that she can avoid having to deal with the fact that her boss has just revealed himself as someone who disregards all the normal workplace boundaries; has just used shocking and inappropriate behavior with her; and has just abused his position – and therefore his power – over her by conducting himself in a way that is designed to embarrass and humiliate her. In handling things this way she chooses not to see the situation for what it is: that her boss is annoyed that she didn't respond immediately to his text requesting that she call him but instead put the ball back into his court two hours later with another text. However, by ignoring his abusive behavior and reducing his bullying to 'a mistake' she mishandles the moment. She fails to use the only source of power available to her in this situation – that of her own reaction to his words – and hands him the initiative.

He seizes the moment and adds insult to injury by reiterating that she must prepare an outline for the following morning's meeting and had better make it a good one. It is eight o'clock at night. She has 13 hours to prepare an outline for a meeting which she hasn't organized, doesn't know anything about and to which he had invited her. It is highly unlikely that she'll be able to produce anything useful and also highly likely that he'll have another go at her in the morning – whatever the quality of her written outline. By failing to take what her boss says to her seriously enough, the PR manager has handed him the power in the relationship and set herself up for a long night and a difficult day ahead. She has also made it easier for him to set a bullying dynamic in motion in the relationship whereby he is abusive and she responds as normal.

The Second Instance: The PR manager does take what her boss says seriously, but doesn't know what to say to him to put the ball back into his court. She lays down a clear boundary by ending the call, hoping that she can at least buy some time to think. Unfortunately for her, her boss calls her straight back and ups the stakes by asking her why she had hung up on him. In her mind she had done no such thing. She was protecting herself against a blatant abuse of power by her boss and a blatant disregard of the boundaries of the relationship by him.

She has the presence of mind to reiterate her position: that she cannot speak with him at that moment and will catch up with him in the office the following day. This is actually quite a clever thing to say, and achieves two things for her. Firstly, it moves the relationship back onto a work footing by telling her boss that they can continue the conversation *in the office*. Secondly, it reinforces her commitment to maintaining what she considers to be appropriate boundaries around their relationship, by letting her boss know that it is too late at night for him to be expecting her to start a new assignment. Her approach tells him quite clearly that she won't speak to him outside office hours if he is going to be inappropriate, but will speak to him at work instead. She has also demonstrated that, even if he calls her back and uses additional verbal force, she will be able to stand her ground. She has successfully thwarted him in his attempt to introduce a bullying dynamic into the relationship this time around, although he is likely to try again in the future.

The Third Instance: The PR manager takes what her boss says very seriously indeed and hears it for what it is: a callous power play designed to intimidate her, confuse her, disrespect all the boundaries in a normal workplace relationship, introduce bogus negative feedback into the mix and set her a spurious assignment to complete within an impossible timescale. She is very alive to these tactics and not at all thrown by them. She makes sure that she is at her most physically powerful stance – standing tall and upright – before speaking, knowing that her tone will reflect her stature. She puts the ball right back into her boss's court telling him that she will need full written particulars of what he considers to be her lack of preparation for the meeting, preferably the following day.

She follows that up with her expectation of him: that as he has set up the meeting, he should lead it. Her boss hears all this and realizes that, as far as this exchange is concerned, he is equally matched. So he softens his tone in an attempt to put her off guard and tells her again that he'd like her to lead the meeting. He attempts to flatter her by telling her that the meeting is important. But she sticks to her guns and reminds him that, as he has set up the meeting, it'd be better for their *employer* if he handled it. There is nothing her boss can do at this juncture but comply, as if he insists that she handle the meeting he will look as if he doesn't have their employer's best interests at heart. Her reaction to the call makes it very clear that this attempt to bully her and this attempt to introduce a bullying dynamic into the relationship, have failed and that she is more than a match for him if he tries again.

Starting to Bully: Conclusions

What conclusions can we come to about the action described above? Firstly, a review of the way the marketing manager handles his PR manager from day one of her employment reveals that something is amiss with him. He is consistently difficult to deal with: he interrupts her when she speaks, doesn't give her airtime, doesn't respond to the points she puts to him, talks over her and at her and makes sure that she has too much to do and no one other than him to talk to about the work. None of this makes him a workplace bully. Rather, it points to one of the two things: either he is a very poor manager indeed or he is deliberately setting her up to fail by giving her too much work and little or no support.

Secondly, we can conclude that, from the moment the PR manager receives her boss's text asking her to call him, her manager's approach to their relationship is moving into different territory. It is unusual for him to text her and ask her to call him. He normally just picks up the phone and dials her number. Of course, it could be a one-off incident: maybe his battery is low and he can only take incoming calls. Whatever the reason for the text, the PR manager is about to go home so, reasonably enough, she waits two hours before responding and when she does she sends him a text rather than risk interrupting his private time by calling him. Her text message tells her boss that she is free and gives him the option of calling her if he wants. To a power-game-playing boss like hers this is a like a red rag to a bull. Even though she didn't intend to, she has incensed him. He sees it as a slight on his status and prestige that she hasn't called him back, but has texted him two hours later giving *him* the option to call *her* if he wants. He rings her to make a furious assault on her as a person and as a professional in two distinct ways:

■ He breaks all the boundaries of a normal workplace relationship by claiming to have been in the shower when her *call* came in. Of course, she didn't call him, she sent him a text: so this is a ploy designed to remind her that he expected her to call him and doesn't like the fact that she didn't. He then tells her that had he a phone that worked in the shower, he would have spoken to her then and there. This is a shocking abuse of power by the marketing manager, one that he hopes will humiliate the PR manager, putting doubts into her mind about him and his intentions toward her, and causing her to feel uncomfortable every time she speaks with him from that point on. This constitutes his powerful attack on her as a person.

■ He then makes an unclear criticism about her approach to preparing for the following day's meeting, a meeting he is in charge of. He tells her that he needs to see her written plans for the meeting on his desk in the morning. This constitutes an attack on her as a professional and is two power plays wrapped up in one: firstly, it is his meeting, one he has set up and therefore would normally handle. His PR manager doesn't know the background to the meeting, who is attending it or what its objectives are and it isn't her job to produce a written outline for it. But he makes it her job anyway. Secondly, he is giving her the assignment out of the blue at eight o'clock at night with a deadline of nine o'clock the following morning. This is an outrageous attempt to set her up to fail, presumably to give him more bogus ammunition with which to attack her the following day.

From the description of the action above we cannot know why the marketing manager decides to use bullying behavior at this moment in his working relationship with the PR manager. We can see that he was always difficult to work with and for, but we do not know what intrapersonal or situational factors have prompted him to take these specific, punishing actions at this juncture. We can clearly see, however, that the PR manager is going to be in for a rough ride unless she stands her ground fairly and squarely for the length of her employment working for this man.

Starting to Bully: Key Lessons

There is no right or wrong way to handle the situation described above. But there are ways to handle it that will prove more beneficial and ways to handle it that will prove less prudent:

- In the first instance the PR manager handles the situation poorly and leaves herself vulnerable to further bullying behavior in future. She doesn't react to her manager's abusive comments, fails to lay down any boundaries in the conversation and fails to create any consequences for her manager to deal with as a result of trying to bully her. Sadly for her she loses power in the relationship, assists her boss in attempting to embed a bullying dynamic into the relationship and hands the initiative to him.
- In the second instance the PR manager handles her boss reasonably well. She protects herself from an abusive call by ending it. She then tells her boss that she isn't available to speak with him until the following morning at work, before ending the call a second time. These actions give him pause for thought and let him know that, if he uses such behavior with her in future, he won't have it all his own way.
- In the third instance, though, the PR manager is at her most assertive and most self-protective. She makes it her job to stay in the conversation with her manager despite his abusive behavior toward her. She clarifies her boundaries and, even though her manager is behaving outrageously, puts the ball right back into his court. She does this in three distinct ways:
  - She uses an assertive and even tone, denoting to her manager that she is not overawed by his tactics but is in charge of both what she is saying and how she is saying it. She tells him – via her tone and

measured, paced verbal delivery – that she and she alone chooses what she says and he does not have the power to throw her off course.

○ She demands written proof of his feedback that she hasn't prepared fully for the following day's meeting. This calls his bluff and, should he decide to write down his concerns – something which isn't at all likely as they are bogus – she will be able to respond to them in a considered fashion, having written evidence of his allegations against her, allegations that she and he both know are unfounded.

○ She reminds him that the following day's meeting is his meeting: he arranged it, he knows the background to it and he knows who else is attending it. It is therefore in his *employer's* interests that he run with the meeting rather than hand it to her. This makes it very difficult for him to try and pass responsibility for the meeting over to her again, unless he wishes to characterize himself as someone who is negligent toward his employer.

■ This approach fully protects her during the call and gives her a very good chance of causing her manager to think again before trying to bully her in the future. She tells him that she won't be intimidated, isn't going to be lightly thrown off course and that, should he continue to use bullying behavior with her, she will handle it and will create consequences for him to deal with. It also tells him that she knows her rights and that, while he might have expectations of her as his employee, she also has expectations of him as a manager.

■ There is no guarantee that her manager won't try a second, third and fourth time to bully her in the days ahead. But he now knows that, should he try, she will not easily give away her power, knows how to protect herself from his abusive tactics and will give as good as she gets. She applies enough pressure to him in this instance that he backs down – for now. She needs to prepare for the possibility that he might be on the attack again, maybe as early as the following morning, but she is now fully alert to the reality of working for him and can make some decisions about how to handle the situation going forward.

CALLING ON YOUR PERSONAL POWER

In this third instance the PR manager does a good job of thwarting her manager in his attempt to introduce a bullying dynamic into their working relationship. She does this by calling on the only source of power available to her at the time – her personal conviction that what her boss is saying and doing is wrong – and successfully counters her boss's superior organizational status. In other words she calls on her personal power to help her resist his greater organizational clout.

So what is personal power and why is it effective at helping her protect herself against her manager's bullying behavior?

Personal power refers to your capacity to choose and remain in charge of your workplace values, choices, actions, decisions, conduct and behavior. Personal power therefore refers to your will or your volitional capacity, and is both individual and personal to you. Calling on your personal power to draw the line is a mightily powerful way of responding to a workplace bully.

Consider the following two further examples:

Example Two: Commanding Attention

A secondary school PE teacher is subject to workplace bullying from the Principal of the school. His bullying takes the form of verbal criticisms and undermining comments to her face, as well as constant interruptions when she speaks at staff meetings. Then he moves his campaign into a new phase and begins undermining her in front of her classes.

He walks onto the tennis courts or into the gym while she is conducting a class and, without waiting for a suitable opportunity, starts to speak to her whether or not she is attending to students. At these times, he simply expects his presence and his voice to result in her stopping what she is doing, cease speaking with her students and give him her full attention. She is so taken aback by his conduct the first time it happens that she does stop what she is doing and does turn toward him. A pattern of behavior is set in motion whereby he commands her attention by his presence in her classes and she acquiesces. He then uses a sarcastic voice to relay to her whatever information he has come to relay, information which is never pressing, urgent or that important. When he has said what he came to say he peremptorily leaves the room without saying goodbye, a behavior which results in the PE teacher feeling humiliated in front of her students.

Fed up of being undermined in front of her class the PE teacher determines to handle the next interview differently. She waits for him to enter the gym and approach her. Before he has a chance to speak she draws herself up to her full height and, turning to face him full on, tells him in a steady, firm and even voice that she is busy with the students but will be with him in a minute. She then turns back to her class and continues from where she had left off. The Principal is thrown and doesn't know how to handle this unexpected turn of events. He is so used to the PE teacher being compliant in the face of his bullying that he doesn't quite know how to handle her new way of doing things. He decides that the best thing to do is to tell her that he will catch her later, which he does before leaving the gym. He doesn't approach her in the middle of class again although he does still interrupt and talk over her in staff meetings.

Commanding Attention: Analyzing the Dynamics

This example features a PE teacher who is naturally respectful toward authority figures. She thinks that it is befitting and proper to show a degree of deference to a more senior member of staff out of respect for their position. To her this is a perfectly normal and natural way to behave and not one that she regards as being either unduly subservient or passive. Unfortunately for her, the Principal of her school is a workplace bully who takes advantage of her goodness and respect for his role. He subjects her to a campaign of bullying, initially carried out to her face and in front of her teaching colleagues, and then also carried out in front of her classes.

Initially she is quite thrown at having such an unpleasant and reprehensible man for a boss. On her own with him, and in front of her colleagues, she is unable to muster the assertive response she needs to protect herself from his belittling and humiliating interruptions and criticisms. However, when he starts to bully her in front of her class she regards this as quite a different matter.

She draws the line at being undermined in front of her students and quickly sets about redressing the balance between them. She uses the fact that the classroom is, as far as she is concerned, her domain to alter her mind-set and summon up the courage to call on an assertive response. She uses behavior which enables her to take control of the situation before the Principal has even spoken and changes the dynamic between them. Her boss is now the one who is vulnerable and initially he doesn't know how to respond to her new mode of dealing with him. He recovers himself and manages to tell her that he will catch her later. Then he leaves the classroom, realizing that the PE teacher might still be naturally respectful toward authority figures, but that that doesn't mean that he will be able to extend his authority unduly into her classroom.

Although she has taken control of matters inside her classroom the PE teacher is still vulnerable to being bullied in front of her colleagues, and to being bullied in one-to-one meetings with the Principal. She will continue to be vulnerable in these environments until she is able to use behavior during these meetings that is as assertive and self-preserving as her approach to handling the Principal in her classes.

Example Three: Snide Comments

A hospital-based nurse is subject to workplace bullying from one of the consultants on her ward. He is snide, picky and unreasonable with her at every opportunity and makes subtly undermining remarks about her to the other staff on the ward, out of her hearing. When he is rude to her face she is often at a loss for what to say back to him. Usually the moment passes without her doing or saying anything in response to his cutting and derogatory comments. She feels intimidated by his status in the hospital – he is a consultant and she is a nurse – and she is disbelieving that someone so senior could behave in such a nasty and personally offensive way to someone who has done him no harm. A pattern of behavior is set in motion between them whereby she remains silent and passive in the face of his bullying verbal behavior.

Fed up of being ridiculed in this way she determines that she will handle him differently and regain some of her self-esteem and personal power. She watches him doing his ward round and then walks toward him when he is not engaged with a patient. She stands by him and waits until he looks at her. Then she tells him in a firm and unwavering tone that she would like to think that he will stop being rude and disrespectful to her face and cease making undermining comments about her behind her back. That is all she says and then she waits for a reply, maintaining level eye contact with him all the while.

The consultant swallows hard. He isn't expecting the nurse to be as steadfast as this or as self-affirming. She hasn't threatened to complain about him or attacked him back. She hasn't whined or used aggressive language or an aggressive tone. She has merely called him to account for his unbecoming conduct and waited for his reply. He doesn't know what to say and feels embarrassed. He starts to tell her she has got it out of all proportion. She interrupts him and tells him in the same even and firm tone that no, that isn't the case and that they both know that what he has been saying is wrong. The consultant doesn't outwardly react to her quiet confrontation. Indeed she doesn't know, from his reaction at the time, that her words have had any impact on him at all. But his bullying behavior does stop and, a few days down the line, she realizes that he is unlikely to pick on her again.

Snide Comments: Analyzing the Dynamics

This example features a nurse who demonstrates great dignity in confronting a consultant about his bullying behavior toward her.

Throughout her interview with him she remains respectful of his position and his authority on the ward, but also makes it clear to him that she is challenging him on his behavior toward her. The consultant initially tries to wriggle out of the situation he finds himself in. He attempts to reduce the level of offense he has caused and to shift blame onto the nurse by telling her that she has 'got it out of all proportion'.

At this point the nurse could have shot herself in the foot. She could have become angry and lost her poise. She could have escalated the discussion into an argument with the consultant. She could have backed down. In any of these instances the nurse would have handed the initiative back to the consultant who would likely have continued with his campaign of bullying.

Instead the nurse maintains her measured, paced style of verbal delivery and regains control of the situation by interrupting the consultant mid-sentence. She does so calmly and with a quiet authority that stuns him. She tells him the fact of the matter: that she hasn't got it out of all proportion and that they both know what he has been saying. By interrupting him to regain control of the conversation, and doing so in such a dignified and self-affirming way, the nurse calls his bluff. The consultant is unmasked and the dynamic between them alters.

Faced with this degree of honesty and poise the consultant is exposed. He doesn't look embarrassed, apologize or speak further to the nurse but his bullying behavior simply stops. It is likely that he picked on the nurse in the first instance because he thought that his authority and position on the ward would mean that she couldn't or wouldn't be able to do anything about his bullying behavior. He assumed, wrongly, that she'd lack the ability to confront him. He thought he would be able to indulge in his habit of bullying her without any comebacks, something which, to his mind, made it a desirable and safe habit to indulge in. In fact he was quite wrong and her quiet confrontation of him is more devastating than any row would have been. She uses her personal conviction that he is out of line to call him to account completely and finally.

FEELING POWERLESS

Having examined a range of choices available to you should you decide to respond assertively to an incident of workplace bullying let's now turn our attention to another facet of the experience of being bullied at work: feeling powerless.

An experience of workplace bullying can leave you feeling power-less. In fact, even one incident of workplace bullying can leave you feeling either powerless or disabled or both. What is so damaging to those of you with firsthand experiences of being bullied – and who relate to feeling powerless at work – is the perception that

- The bully is inter–personally and/or organizationally more powerful than you.
- You don't know how to act in ways which will prevent the bully from bullying you again.

This dual whammy can leave you feeling, quite literally, overwhelmed and can prevent you, just like the PR manager in the first instance, from acting in your own best interests at the time you most need to. Specifically, it can leave you feeling that you don't know what to do to:

- Prevent a further incident of bullying.
- Protect yourself from any subsequent incidents of bullying.
- Persuade your employers to enforce action against the person bullying you.

It is frightening to feel both powerless and in danger. It can sap your will, and leave you feeling alone and vulnerable. Even if you want very much to take steps to handle your situation effectively you might simply not know what to do and you might conclude that there isn't much you can do to alter the situation you find yourself in. For any adult at work these alternatives are very unpleasant prospects indeed.

Faced with these realities many people subject to workplace bully-ing use behavior which is outwardly compliant, accommodating and submissive at the time they are being bullied. They are unaware that these are the very reactions that workplace bullies thrive off.

REFRAMING WORKPLACE BULLYING AS A SERIES OF ABUSIVE INTERACTIONS

However, even if it doesn't *feel* like it, handling workplace bullying well is about responding effectively to a series of individual instances of bullying behavior; and, in some cases, it is about responding effec-tively to only one incident of bullying behavior. Seen in this light it might appear to be a more manageable experience.

Resisting a workplace bully is about handling a series of interactions with the person who wants to bully you until they learn to:

- Cease bullying you altogether.

Or:

- Reduce the potency and frequency of their abusive behavior to more manageable levels.

That's it.

Depending on the circumstances you find yourself in, some of you might only need to handle one instance of bullying behavior effectively before the bully gets the message and desists. Others of you might be called on to handle more than one incident of bullying behavior effectively before your assailant ceases their activity. The incidents you need to handle might be spaced out by a few minutes, a few hours or a few days and weeks depending on how often you and the workplace bully interact with one another.

Whichever way it falls, your job is to mentally prepare for the next interaction with the person bullying you – even though you most likely won't be able to predict exactly when that interaction will occur – and handle it in the most self-preserving and self-protective way you can. Your aim is to give the bully the consistent and clear message that you will do this until they realize that they are not going to prevail against you and choose to stop using bullying behavior when dealing with you.

Some of your interactions with the bully will go well, others less well. But, overall, your job is to send back the consistent message to the bully that, if they continue to subject you to bullying behavior, you will resist them and will go on resisting them until they choose to stop bullying you or reduce their bullying activity to manageable levels. Very few workplace bullies will continue to bully someone who is a match for their tactics and who behaves in a way which denotes that they are neither intimidated by them, controlled by them, thrown by them nor submissive in the face of their aggression.

Some bullies will get the message very quickly indeed. Others may need a bit more time to learn the reality that they are outmatched – or at least equally matched. It's a learning curve for you and for them. But it is a learning curve that you can climb if you want to. It is a question of your will.

CHOOSING NOT TO RESIST

However, all that said, it's still your choice whether or not you decide to climb the learning curve and resist a workplace bully. Those of you who doubt that you can muster the resolve to try and handle bullying behavior effectively simply don't have to. It is up to you to decide whether or not you want to. Only you can decide what is right for you given the interpersonal and intrapersonal resources you have left, and the support available to you inside and outside your workplace.

You might have little or no mental strength left. You might feel so crushed that you cannot think. You might consider it beyond you to stand your ground in your next meeting with the person bullying you. Resisting a workplace bully is a choice and you may feel that it isn't the right choice for you. However, if you decide to keep your head down and cope with it you could also consider:

- Making a formal complaint so that other people get involved.
- Seeking alternative employment elsewhere.

Should you choose not to resist *and* remain unsupported in an abusive situation you might risk sliding into depression. In this situation you could consider obtaining professional advice from a therapist, psychologist or health professional skilled at working with people subject to workplace bullying. You don't simply have to stay put and let your self-esteem be further damaged and your energy and vitality be further drained.

Consider the following example:

Example Four: Losing Power

A strategist is headhunted from a university research unit to work in the oil industry assessing the environmental risk inherent in opening up new offshore oil fields. He is asked to run a team of eight people, all skilled and experienced professionals. He is delighted to be approached for the job but has some reservations about taking a role in industry after working in an academic environment for so many years. He is particularly worried that his more toned down style won't cut it in the robust and raw environment of an oil company. But, in the end, he decides that the new challenge and experience will be beneficial for him and he accepts the post.

After four months he thinks he might have made a big mistake. His boss doesn't see much value in his low-key, methodical style, and doesn't consult him on important decisions anymore. His key peers don't either and he has little influence around the office or with the field crew. He regularly gets left out of information-giving and decision-making loops and is worried that his upcoming appraisal will not be positive. His team doesn't like what they see as his controlling and pedantic style. In his heart of hearts he knows that things haven't gone well for him but he also knows that the more aggressive, and as he sees it, action-oriented style of his key office contacts isn't one that he will easily be able to replicate.

Then events take a nasty turn. One of his key office contacts, an influential peer who has been employed by the oil company for years, starts to use bullying behavior with him. Over a three-week period she escalates her bullying until she makes an outright attack on his competency. Initially she uses a cold and cutting tone during telephone calls with him. Then she starts to come over to his desk and use unnecessary verbal force with him. Finally, she sends him a curt e-mail, copied to everyone in the office, in which she describes his interim report as 'ill-thought out', 'ill-considered' and 'fundamentally flawed'. The strategist is shocked and shaken by the e-mail. As someone who prides himself on the quality of both his thinking and his written work he cannot believe that someone could write such a damning review of his latest report and copy it to everyone in the office without so much as discussing it with him first. He is confident enough in his work to stand by his report and thinks that her comments are purely designed to humiliate him. He feels very angry, so angry that he marches straight over to her desk which is in the adjoining open plan office.

In the altercation which follows, the strategist handles himself poorly. He is visibly shaken both by his own anger and by the fact that he is displaying it publically at work, something he has never done before. His peer remains seated behind her desk during the entire interview and seems amused by his discomfort. She refuses to apologize to him, tone down her e-mail or withdraw it from circulation. He leaves her desk defeated and humiliated and goes home.

His peer continues to bully him, now more confident than ever that her tactics unhinge him and make him wobble. She enjoys watching the unnerving effect she has on him and takes pleasure in her ability to upset him. She is rude to him whenever she sees him calling him 'computer code' or 'robot man'. She physically bumps into him in the corridor and walks away without speaking to him. She interrupts him every time he ventures an opinion at meetings making sure that she gives a contrary or opposing view. Her colleagues watch these antics with wry amusement but no one offers any advice or support to the hapless strategist.

Two months later, at his half-yearly appraisal, his argument with his peer is a key topic of discussion, and is used as evidence against him by his boss who tells him that he doesn't 'know how to handle himself around the office'. Six weeks later, having failed to establish the credibility he would have liked, he decides that enough is enough and resigns. He is fortunate to be offered a return to his former role in academia, a role he gladly accepts.

Losing Power: Analyzing the Dynamics

Let's examine the choices made by the strategist during this unfortunate episode in his working life.

Firstly, he decides to leave an environment to which he is well suited – a university – and a role at which he is adept and well-respected – a research unit – and join a robust and action-oriented oil company. On the face of it this is a risk, but it's a risk that he assesses and thinks worth the gamble. In making this choice the strategist thinks he has a better than even chance of winning over his new colleagues to the merits of his more low-key style but, sadly for him, he doesn't manage to. He quickly finds that neither his boss nor his peers have time for his way of doing things and he quickly starts to lose both credibility and influence around the office. In fact, it is probably true to say that he experiences the culture of his new employer as one in which his strengths – a methodical, thoughtful, quality-conscious style – are routinely characterized as weaknesses and are regarded as slow, unimaginative and unpersuasive. At this point, just when he could do with some support and a boost to his confidence, one of his key peers starts to use bullying behavior when she deals with him.

At this critical point the strategist makes a second series of poor choices. He doesn't do anything to defend himself when he becomes subject to her bullying behavior. In fact initially he fails to react to it at all. He doesn't object or assert himself, partly because he doesn't know how to – it's not in his nature – and partly because he thinks the actions his peer is taking against him are unprofessional, so he ignores them. Rather than lower himself to her level by pushing back when she bullies him he pays no attention to her abuse and carries on as normal, hoping she'll get bored of the game and desist. Unfortunately for him she doesn't get bored – she gets more aggressive. She eventually attacks his work publically and only then does she get a reaction from him.

It is doubtful that she bullies him solely to get a reaction from him. But it is likely that his lack of response to her bullying behavior encourages her to bully him more, if only because he fails to make her face any consequences for using such an approach: his failure to react means that she doesn't have to think again. Instead of responding assertively and giving her pause for thought, the strategist is irate with his peer in front of a room full of their colleagues. Only some of these people would know of her tactics against him; and only some of them would have read the e-mail at the time they witness the altercation. What they do see is him being unreasonably angry with her and her sitting calmly behind her desk. He is unused to expressing emotion at work, and having entered unfamiliar emotional territory, cannot readily handle a situation which he has unwittingly created: a public, volatile row with a colleague well used to conflict. His colleague is very comfortable indeed with her own emotions and has no difficulty deflecting his. In fact she doesn't even move from behind her desk during the altercation.

Thirdly, at the height of the argument, when he is on the back foot and his foe is very much to the fore, the strategist makes another series of foolish choices. He asks his peer for an apology for sending the e-mail which offended him. She refuses so he asks for a retraction of it which she also refuses. He finally asks her to resend a softened version of the original e-mail. She refuses that request too leaving him with nothing to do but to walk away from her desk embarrassed and defeated. In asking a bullying peer to admit wrongdoing, the strategist has shot himself in the foot. In his mind her actions were indefensible and, given the opportunity to redress them, he assumed that she would readily do so. He assumed that she would want to see the error of her ways and welcome an opportunity to make amends. He completely misjudges her character and her motives. Furthermore, his requests only serve to strengthen her hand and weaken him further.

Fourthly, when her bullying of him becomes even more puerile after the public row he still fails to champion his own cause. He doesn't react at all to her tactics in subsequent meetings or in corridors, allowing her bullying to continue unopposed. In his mind her actions are too childish to warrant a response from him. In reality, he doesn't know what to do and worries that, should he try and take her on again, it would be as disastrous for him as when he confronted her at her desk. He feels that right is on his side, but his self-justification doesn't defend him against her constant workplace bullying.

Finally, he does make a self-preserving choice and he decides to leave the oil company. He is able to return to his former post at the university, an environment where his style is appreciated and where the accepted ways of behaving are in line with his own values. He has a good chance of finding healing from the effects of workplace bullying which are both intrapersonal to him – the loss of his self-confidence and self-esteem – and interpersonal – the loss of credibility and respect of his coworkers.

Losing Power: Conclusions

What conclusions can we draw from this example? Firstly, we can empathize considerably with the horrible situation in which the strategist finds himself. He is given a considerable ego boost by being headhunted for a role by a new employer. But he quickly finds that he doesn't fit in and that his low-key style is misunderstood and characterized as being ineffective by his more combatively minded colleagues.

Secondly, we can also empathize with the fact that, at the time he becomes subject to workplace bullying, the strategist feels friendless at work and is at a low point. He doesn't have the emotional or intrapersonal resources to fight back and, lacking interpersonal support at work, can't muster a shot back in anger at his more powerful and well-connected peer. This is a very trying set of circumstances indeed but, nonetheless, it is the situation in which he finds himself and it is one which he needs to handle well to avoid an ignominious exit.

What could he have done to preserve his boundaries, retain his personal power and interrupt what becomes a wearisome bullying dynamic between him and his peer? Here are some options he could have pursued:

- He could have made an early decision to leave the oil company – perhaps before he becomes subject to workplace bullying. This is a difficult choice indeed to exercise but it is one he could have seriously considered as soon as he realized that his characteristic ways of getting things done would not be supported or understood in his new employer's culture. He could have decided that the differences in values between him and his new colleagues are so great that it'd be better for him to leave than stay and continue to lose credibility, influence and self-confidence. As someone used to workplace success the strategist isn't equipped to cope with this potent combination of losses and his self-esteem plummets as a result.
- He could have reacted more effectively to the initial bullying tactics used by his peer. He doesn't react at all to her cold and cutting telephone calls. Neither does he react to her face-to-face forcefulness. His failure to say anything to her in response to her cutting tone, coupled with her persistence in using bullying behavior, sets up a dynamic in which she ups the stakes and uses more and more aggressive behavior with him and he simply lets her do so unopposed. Why does she up the stakes? Firstly, because he doesn't do anything to dissuade her from this course of action; and secondly, because she can. She sees it as a challenge to get him to react. And eventually he does react: quite explosively.

- He could have handled her blatantly provocative e-mail quite differently, in a way that played to his strengths and avoided an encounter with her at her desk, something which exposed his vulnerabilities. He could have replied to her points by e-mailing everyone on the circulation list including her with a measured, written rebuttal to each of them. This approach would have played to his strengths of cool, reasoned argument and he would have had an opportunity to tell the entire circulation list what he thought of her attempt to discredit his report. This approach would have meant that, at the very least, his peer would have been openly exposed and put in her place and everyone on the circulation list would have had an opportunity to recognize this fact. The strategist would have needed to word his e-mail carefully using a dispassionate and factual tone, but he takes another path instead, allowing his anger to fog his mind. He confronts someone who is very comfortable with conflict, in an open plan office. He gets soundly beaten even though right is on his side, and his bullying peer continues with her campaign against him unopposed by him or anyone else.
- Lastly, he could have laid down a marker every time his peer bullies him in a meeting or in the corridor after the verbal altercation at her desk. When she knocks into him in the corridor he could have stated the fact calmly and clearly: 'you've just bumped into me'. His tone would need to contain a degree of incredulous anger that she could do such a thing and not acknowledge it. By saying nothing he avoids a necessary conflict, loses credibility and perpetuates the cycle of abuse. After she interrupts him in meetings he needs to assert himself, look straight at her and say firmly and clearly, 'before I was interrupted I was saying that…'. Then he needs to finish his point making eye contact with each of the people at the meeting in turn and using a very firm tone which challenges anyone to interrupt him again. Finally, when his peer calls him insulting names he needs to respond immediately. He could say: 'my name is…' or 'wrong again!' In a way it doesn't matter what he says as long as he does say *something* and in a tone that conveys his feelings to her. These actions will regain a measure of control for him in abusive situations and give her the message that he will not disregard her behavior toward him but will pick up on it and respond to it as and when it happens.

Once he joins the oil company the strategist's choices are limited. But, had he exercised them differently, he could have protected himself from a difficult and sustained series of blows to his confidence and stood up to a pernicious workplace bully more effectively.

SUMMARY AND NEXT CHAPTER

This chapter has examined the issues and behaviors involved in resisting a workplace bully. It has clarified how to manage your boundaries and draw on your personal power to protect yourself from bullying behavior. The chapter has suggested that choosing to resist a bully is as valid a choice as choosing not to resist a bully, although not resisting carries risks with it. The chapter has incorporated a series of examples to illustrate how to respond assertively to bullying behavior, and has demonstrated the pitfalls of responding from anger rather than measured assertion.

The chapter has:

- Highlighted how to call on your personal power to send back clear messages to a workplace bully that you know how to protect yourself and are equipped to respond assertively.
- Identified the key role that effective management of your boundaries plays when you are subject to bullying behavior.
- Illustrated how people who are being bullied can inadvertently help their assailant to establish a bullying dynamic in the relationship by giving their power away or by failing to preserve it.
- Acknowledged that, for some of you, not resisting a workplace bully might be the best way to preserve what resources and energy you have left.

The next chapter changes tack. It focuses on the challenges facing those of you who think that one of your team members might be consistently using bullying behavior, and realize that the task of confronting their behavior falls to you. It highlights how to go about this responsibility effectively so that you stand a good chance of influencing your team member to cease using bullying behavior.

CHAPTER 6

Managing a Workplace Bully
Confronting Bullying Behavior in a Team Member

In this chapter we'll be considering your options as a manager who thinks that they might have a workplace bully in their team. The chapter will examine your role as the person whose responsibility it is to:

- Recognize that you have a team member who is using bullying behavior.
- Establish whether or not they are consistently using bullying behavior and are in fact a workplace bully – or whether they use aggression on an occasional or infrequent basis.
- Confront a bullying team member about their ongoing use of coercive behavior.
- Manage the situation to a satisfactory conclusion.

This chapter will explore the pitfalls you'd do well to avoid as you undertake these tasks. It will highlight how your bullying team member might react to you should you decide to confront them. It will identify the various strategies that they might use to avoid responsibility for their actions. It will illustrate the obfuscations and justifications they might use to cloud the real issues; and the real blindness they might have to the consequences of their actions for those they bully, for themselves, for their future careers and for you as their manager.

The aim of this chapter is to steer you away from less productive – although quite understandable – ways of handling a confrontation with a workplace bully and toward more profitable ways of handling the interview. It will also present those of you who shy away from the responsibility of speaking with a bullying team member with the reality of what it means for the people who they continue to target, if you take this line.

The objectives of this chapter are to:

- Establish the fact that managers in every organization have a responsibility to act when they see workplace bullying occurring.

- Identify common pitfalls that managers can fall into when doing this.
- Illustrate some of the tactics a bullying team member might employ to avoid responsibility for their actions when you confront them – and what to do should this happen.
- Outline ways in which to tackle a bullying team member effectively over their behavior.

YOUR CHALLENGE AS A MANAGER OF A BULLY

Workplace bullies use behavior which injures other people at work. When confronted with this fact most bullies will deny that it is true. They will deny that their actions actually hurt anyone and will most likely try and deflect the conversation on to a related issue such as how:

- The people they target are underperforming and need pushing to get them into gear.
- They are struggling to meet their targets because the quality of people they have been given to work with isn't good enough.
- The manager confronting them is mistaken – they've got the wrong end of the stick or someone has been complaining about them unjustifiably.
- They have been promoted (or hired) precisely because of the fact that they use behavior which gets results – and to penalize them now is nonsense from their point of view.

Some workplace bullies genuinely don't recognize the harm they do to others. They don't consciously want to hurt anyone else. They often have very low levels of emotional self-awareness and little ability to empathize with other people's feelings. They often claim that they don't understand how their bullying behavior can upset people – and, sadly, sometimes this is true: they don't.

Other workplace bullies do recognize that they give other people a hard time and that they 'pick on' selected people. But they convince themselves that the upset they cause is either fleeting, doesn't really count or is deserved by those on the receiving end. With such levels of denial and blindness how do you, as a manager, go about convincing a workplace bully that they need to reappraise their conduct and start to use a completely different – and as yet undeveloped – interpersonal skill-set?

Your challenge as the manager of a workplace bully is to do just that. Your job – once you are sure that you have a bully in your team – is to act in ways that convey the consistent message to the bully that their bullying behavior:

- Isn't acceptable.
- Must stop.
- Needs to be replaced with effective people-handling skills.

Consider the following example:

Example One: Bad Hire

The Sales Director of a chain of retail stores decides that he spends too much time in the office working with his able office-based team. His style of managing the team is one they really appreciate. He devolves responsibility to them, gives them genuine autonomy and provides them with training and support when they need it. He is well-liked and respected by all of the people who work for him.

He decides that he wants to change the way in which he manages his time and works with his team. He determines to hire a Project Manager to coordinate and manage office-based sales activity and provide him with the option of spending more time in the retail stores, setting new and challenging sales targets for the staff who work in them. After an extensive interview process he hires an ambitious woman in her mid-40s to run his office-based team for him. He thinks that she is quite a tough operator but that she has considerable experience in retails sales and sales management. The Sales Director is optimistic that she'll make a positive contribution to his department when he leaves the office in her hands. He spends three days with her in the office introducing her to the team, their current workload and their project schedule and then undertakes a tour of the store outlets across the country, a process that takes him just over three weeks. Then he returns to the office and finds that things have changed.

The first thing he notices is how downbeat everyone is. He has an office-based team of 12, all bright and enthusiastic sales people. On entering the open plan office at 8.30 in the morning, after his countrywide tour of the stores, he is surprised that only one other person is in the room before him. Usually between three and six people could be counted on to arrive by 8.30 in the morning. By 9 o'clock all 12 people and the Project Manager are in the office, but the usual buzz is lacking. Rather than a hive of activity, the atmosphere is low key – even sullen – and several ebullient people are simply sitting at their desks with their heads down. The Sales Director thinks something is wrong and calls the Project Manager into his office.

Over the next two days the Sales Director begins to suspect that the Project Manager's style is having an adverse effect around the office. He observes her using a harsh and cutting tone with two of the more junior members of staff and notices that, after one-to-one meetings with her in a side-office, individual members of staff seem dejected. He decides to speak to his longest-serving staff member and asks her to come to his office. Her sits her down and, quite straightforwardly, asks her how the team is responding to the new Project Manager. He expects that he'll be given a candid answer. He has known this particular team member for years and they work well together. He simply assumes that he'll get a straight answer to a straight question.

There are a number of ways in which this staff member could respond to the situation she finds herself in when she is asked by the Sales Director how the team is responding to the Project Manager. Let's examine three of them:

- She wants very much to tell her boss about the kinds of behavior which she has experienced and has witnessed the new Project Manager using with the team. She likes the Sales Director and has worked with him for a long time but she is also wary of the situation she finds herself in. He did hire the Project Manager and she doesn't know just how much the Sales Director will want to hear the truth about the behavior of his hire around the office. So she decides to be cautious and, when asked what she thinks of the Project Manager, says that the team is still adjusting to her style.

- She is wary of upsetting the apple cart, very aware indeed that the Sales Director wants to spend time away from the office, in the stores, from now on, and clear that he needs to feel that he can do so with the office left in good hands. She doesn't have the courage to tell her boss that the Project Manager is a bully and regularly uses verbal force and coercive behavior with her team members. So she tells the Sales Director that the new Project Manager is challenging to work for but gets results. Then she says she has plenty to be getting on with and suggests that she get back to work.

- She is not at all keen to have a conversation about the Project Manager behind her back. While she has no doubt that the Sales Director is genuinely keen to get to the bottom of the changed atmosphere in the office, she is also clear that he will be tied up at a Board off-site for the rest of the week and that she'll be in the office with the Project Manager. She worries that if she says anything to her boss, he will take it up with the Project Manager before the close of the day, no doubt paving the way for reprisals the following day.

She decides to keep quiet and merely tells him that they are getting used to the style of the new Project Manager and that she thinks it'll work out fine.

Bad Hire: Analyzing the Dynamics

Let's take a look at what is happening in these three scenarios starting with the first one:

The First Instance: The team member wants very much to spill the beans about the Project Manager's bullying behavior but she has a number of concerns about doing so. She is very aware that the Sales Director has hired the Project Manager and that he'd naturally have decided that she would be capable of doing a good job before he offered her the position. She knows the Sales Director quite well – but not well enough to know for sure that he would want to hear the truth about his poor judgment in hiring her. She is concerned that the way the Project Manager must have presented herself at the interview, and in her subsequent dealings with the Sales Director, is likely to be very different from how she does things when he isn't in the office. She thinks the Sales Director might not believe her if she tells it like it is.

However, she is also conscious of her responsibility to the rest of the team. For all she knows, if the Sales Director is out of the office a lot from now on, this chat might be the only opportunity any of them will have to tell the Sales Director what's going on behind his back – and responsibility for handling this opportunity well has fallen to her. So she tests the water with her comment that the team is adjusting to her style.

She says this to create an opening for the Sales Director should he wish to find out more. She hopes that the Sales Director will ask further well-judged, carefully posed questions. He could ask her 'in what way does her style need adjusting to?' or simply say 'tell me more'. If he does, the team member will need to decide just how much she wants to say, and will also need to form a view, based on how he asks his questions, about just how much discretion he will use from that point onward. They are both in a tricky position: the team member because she will be in the line of fire for the rest of the week if the Sales Director mishandles any potential meeting with his Project Manager before the end of the day; the Sales Director because it will be embarrassing for him to realize that he has hired a manager with few managerial skills and with a propensity to bully her staff.

The Second Instance: The team member doesn't feel able to tell the Sales Director what has been happening in his absence and decides to avoid having the conversation she needs to have with him. She thinks there is too much at stake from her manager's point of view for her to risk telling it like it is. She misguidedly decides to protect her boss from the truth about his bad hire, tells him that the Project Manager is challenging to work for but gets results, and hastily leaves his office. She is in a tricky position but by handling things this way she hasn't helped herself or her team colleagues, and has prevented the Sales Director from hearing the bad news that he needs to hear.

The Third Instance: The team member is very concerned that, should she tell the Sales Director what has been going on, she will be the target for a sustained period of bullying during the rest of the week when the Sales Director is away from the office. She can't face the prospect of being singled out in this way and decides to protect herself from that possibility by covering up the truth. Faced with a conflict between telling the truth and being left vulnerable to renewed bullying, and hiding the truth in the hope of containing the bullying at its current level, she makes her choice. She says that the Project Manager is tough to work for but everything will work out fine, and gives the Sales Director nothing to work with.

Bad Hire: Conclusions

What conclusions can we come to about the action described above? Firstly, a review of the way in which the Project Manager handles the selection interview process and her subsequent conduct around the office tells us that she is skilled at manipulating the Sales Director's perceptions. To the Sales Director's face she presents herself as capable, effective and experienced. She convinces him that she is knowledgeable about sales, skilled at handling people and committed to carrying on his good work, as a result of which she secures a job and a place of trust in his team. Behind his back the façade drops and she reveals herself as a workplace bully: someone without effective people-handling skills and with a penchant for routinely using punishing, coercive behavior with everyone in her team.

Secondly, we can conclude that the Sales Director is no fool. He quickly picks up on the fact that something fundamental has changed around the office and takes action to find out what. But he mishandles the interview he has with his longest-serving team member and thereby complicates the situation. He fails to realize just how far things have gone in three weeks and doesn't recognize how intimidated she and the other team members feel. She doesn't want to speak up about what is going on, fearing subsequent encounters with the Project Manager. She doesn't know enough about the Sales Director's attitude to workplace bullying or his sensitivity in handling the issues the team now faces to be able to trust him with the truth. She worries that he wouldn't want to hear the fact of the matter because it compromises his judgment in having hired the Project Manager in the first place.

Thirdly, we can conclude that, having recognized that something is wrong around the office, and having failed to get to the bottom of it in his first meeting on the subject, the Sales Director cannot afford to make another mistake. The situation he returns to after three weeks away is one where his team is already looking like a group of people who don't enjoy their work, probably aren't performing as effectively as they used to, and may be, in some cases, considering other employment options. He has to get his next move right if he is to retain the buoyant, productive and enjoyable team he has worked so hard to create.

We will return to this situation later on in the chapter to see how it progresses but for now let's spend some time assessing the character of the new Project Manager and the Sales Director:

Character Cameo One: The Project Manager

The Project Manager is an experienced sales professional but isn't good at managing people. She is used to working in highly structured work environments where her lack of people-handling skills didn't matter that much. But, in the Sales Director's unstructured office-based team, she is exposed almost immediately as someone without real people-handling ability. She doesn't know how to handle her interpersonally able and adept team members and bullies them out of her fear that she isn't as competent at her job as they are at theirs.

The Project Manager does have plenty of experience in sales and plenty of knowledge about retail businesses. During her selection interviews with the Sales Director, she easily convinces him that she knows what she is talking about. However, his selection process does not include any effective test of her claim that she possesses well-developed people-handling skills. She talks with him about how she would handle various challenging interpersonal situations that the Sales Director describes to her – but he never sees her in action. The selection process allows her to cover up her lack of real ability with people while enabling her to make it sound as if she possesses a well-developed toolkit in this area.

Almost from day one she is on the back foot. Filling the popular Sales Director's shoes as day-to-day manager of the team is a big job for her and one she isn't up to. She doesn't know how to build rapport with his team members, doesn't easily trust them and worries from day one about the possibility of failure. She *feels* incompetent to handle the challenge of managing this group of people and realizes that her knowledge base alone will not be enough to cover up for her interpersonal inadequacies. She quickly starts to use bullying and coercive behavior. She thinks that if they don't like her – something which she fears more than knows – then the team will at least respect her, so she sets about driving them hard.

None of her fears or worries excuses her bullying behavior. She bullies everyone in the team and is especially punishing with people in one-to-one meetings away from the gaze of their colleagues in the open plan office. Deep down she knows that she can never compete with the leadership skills and personality of the Sales Director; but, rather than concentrate on diligent and effective management of the team, she starts to scapegoat them in an attempt to feel better about herself and to punish *them* for *her* inadequacies as a manager.

Character Cameo Two: The Sales Director

The Sales Director is an able leader: he builds effective relationships with his team and is willing to give them both autonomy and support, a powerful combination which enables his independent-minded workforce to thrive. His team members like him and enjoy working for him. He has created an effective, consistently high-performing team and is also a good man who wouldn't knowingly place his team in the hands of a bully. After three weeks out of the office, a period of time in which he leaves his team to the care of the Project Manager, he quickly notices a significant change for the worse among his members of staff.

Having realized that something is up he now faces several conflicts. Firstly, he wants to continue to work away from the office for a large part of each week. He can only do this if he leaves someone in charge of the team. At the moment, that person is the Project Manager. If she isn't up to the role then he will have to find a replacement for her or give added responsibility to one of his existing office-based team members. Making these decisions and carrying out the time-consuming work around them will inevitably take up his time when he wants to be doing other things.

Secondly, he hired the Project Manager and so has a vested interest in her succeeding in her new role. He is capable of changing his mind about a team member's supposed competence and isn't the sort to blind himself to the reality of his own mistakes. But he needs convincing that something serious enough to warrant his action has happened since the Project Manager took over day-to-day management of the team, and he is struggling to get the evidence he needs to verify his suspicions.

Thirdly, he has begun to implement his plans for a big increase in sales targets around the stores. He does not want to have to put his plans on hold so soon after starting them but will not be able to bring them to fruition without having someone to manage the office day-to-day. He hasn't really considered any of his existing team members for the job and, if he decides that it isn't working out with the Project Manager, he might have to contemplate putting his plans on hold while he replaces her.

All that said, he would like to get to the bottom of why the atmosphere in the office has changed so much, why it is that certain of his team members look resentful and browbeaten, and why the general morale of the team has taken an obvious dip.

* * *

Having assessed the character of the two key sales managers in this example let's now return to the action and see what happens next:

Example Two: Confrontation

The Sales Director returns from the Board off-site to a gloomy and despondent office. He determines to try a second time to find out what is amiss with the team. He arranges a series of one-to-one meetings with the four most experienced members of his team, including the woman with whom he spoke first. He holds these interviews in a private meeting room on a Monday morning during a week in which he will be in office all week. He starts each meeting by saying that he has noticed that the atmosphere in the office has changed and seems downbeat. He also says that he'd like to have a candid conversation which will remain confidential. He then asks his team member what has been going on and keeps asking until he gets some answers.

On completing the four meetings with his team members the Sales Director then arranges to meet with the Project Manager in a meeting room. He starts by saying that he is pleased to have an opportunity to catch up with her after a hectic last few weeks and asks her how it is going. The Project Manager replies that things are going well and asks if there is anything specific that the Sales Director wants to speak with her about. He says there is and outlines how he has noticed a dip in energy levels and morale among the team over the last few weeks and that it is concerning him. He asks her if she can shed any light on it.

There are a number of ways in which the Project Manager could respond to this situation. Let's examine three of them:

- The Project Manager tells the Sales Director that she is concerned at the quality of some of her members of staff. She outlines two incidents in which she said she felt the need to pull team members up on their shoddy work, and two more in which she said that team members were 'messing about in the office' instead of working hard. She characterizes the named team members in question as people who don't act quickly enough, clearly enough or with sufficient decisiveness. She makes sure that three of them are among the group of people she knows has already spoken with the Sales Director that morning in private conversations. She says they need too much direction and hand-holding and she isn't used to having to work with such dithering people. She then says that she finds the team in general to be staffed by wishy-washy people, more interested in 'being nice' to one another than getting on and doing the job in hand. The Sales Director struggles in his mind to square up this description of people he has worked with for a long time with his experience of them. He sees them as able, confident and capable, not indecisive and weak. In the silence that accompanies his thoughts on these issues the Project Manager tells him that he has been soft on them and has bred into them a 'dependence on him' which is unhealthy. She tells him that she wants 'to shake them up a bit' and wean them off him. The Sales Director is amazed at this allegation and, for a moment, simply doesn't know what to say. The Project Manager tells him that she needs to return to her urgent work. She leaves the room and goes back to her desk.
- The Project Manager denies that there is a problem with the team. She says that they are working hard and getting on with their jobs. She asks the Sales Director what he is getting at. He replies that he has concerns about the atmosphere in the office, saying it is very different from a month ago and that he'd like to understand what has happened in the intervening period. The Project Manager tells him that the atmosphere in the team isn't the issue that he should be concerning himself with, but that the team's performance is. She tells him that the team is on track to meet its quarterly goals and that she'd like to get back to work as she has some urgent matters to attend to. She then stands up and, looking the Sales Director in the eye, tells

him that he hired her precisely for her qualities as a manager and to question her approach now seems to suggest woolly thinking on his part. Without waiting for an answer she leaves the meeting room.

- The Project Manager looks the Sales Director in the eye and says, in an indignant tone, that if anyone has spoken 'out of turn' about her she'd like to know who said what. She bristles angrily. The Sales Director is worried at the turn the meeting has taken so early on but perseveres. He replies that he'd prefer to get the Project Manager's perspective on the situation. The Project Manager angrily asks 'what situation?' and the Sales Director reiterates that he is concerned about the dip in morale being exhibited by many members of the team. The Project Manager replies that her boss shouldn't be listening to slander and should be congratulating her for having held the fort so successfully in his absence. She repeats that she has a 'right to know' if anyone has been talking about her behind her back and glares back at the Sales Director. He tells her that he wants to speak with her about *his* concerns and would like to understand why the team members seem downbeat and dejected. The Project Manager says, in an angry tone, that they are not downbeat and dejected but are working hard at the tasks she has assigned to them. The Sales Director wants to pursue his concerns but decides that the level of emotion being exhibited by the Project Manager will make it difficult to make progress this time round. Reluctantly, he ends the meeting.

Confrontation: Analyzing the Dynamics

Let's take a look at what is happening in these three scenarios starting with the first one:

The First Instance: The Project Manager questions both the competence and the character of several members of the team, before questioning the values of everyone in it and the Sales Director for breeding an unhealthy dependence into his team members. This is a ploy designed to take the conversation away from the issues which the Sales Director wants to discuss with her and into completely different territory. By questioning the team members' conduct, the Project Manager hopes to put doubts about them into his mind. She hopes that this attack will deflect his attention away from her impact on the team and onto the inadequacies, as she sees it, of the team members. She has no hesitation in characterizing people the Sales Director has worked with for years and knows well, as 'wishy-washy'. She makes her claims in a clear, firm voice and hopes to knock the Sales Director out of his stride, perhaps even turning the tables on him.

She succeeds because while he is trying to get to grips with her characterization of the team members as weak and needy, she blames him for mismanaging the team and creating an unhealthy dynamic between them and him. The Sales Director has not seen himself or his team in this light before and needs time to process what he is being told, before he can respond. She hopes to destabilize his high-quality relationships with his team members by questioning his ability to manage them, characterizing it as being about 'creating dependence' on him among them. She hopes this attack will confuse him and that, as a result, he will pull away from them giving her more room to maneuver. Her attack comes from envy: deep down she'd love to achieve the trusting and spontaneous relationships with her team colleagues that the Sales Director has built. But she is unable to and so, rather than concentrate on working on addressing her own interpersonal skills deficits and intrapersonal issues, she chips away at his great strength – that of connecting with people – and characterizes it as 'unhealthy'.

To some extent the Project Manager succeeds in bamboozling the Sales Director into losing his way in the conversation. In the silence during which he is thinking about what to say next, the Project Manager takes the opportunity to offer her final salvo. She tells him that she is going to 'wean' the team members off him before smartly leaving the room and returning to the open plan office. This is her way of telling him that she expects to handle the team from now on and will take steps to make sure that she does so without interference from him. She hopes that this tactic will dissuade the Sales Director from wanting to reopen this conversation again but, if he does, she will be ready for him and will return to the attack again.

The Second Instance: The Project Manager keeps the interview very short indeed. She volunteers no information at all to the Sales Director, doesn't answer his questions and characterizes him as wasting her time and woolly headed. The first contribution she makes to the meeting is to tell her boss that the team is performing to target and that she'd like to get back to work. This strategy is designed to pull the rug from under the Sales Director's feet, switching the point of the conversation from his choice of the unhealthy atmosphere in the team to a topic of her choice: the fact that the team she is managing is performing to target. This makes it very difficult for the Sales Director to proceed with his line of enquiry as to do so would leave him looking misguided.

In the silence that follows the Project Manager claims that she has urgent matters to attend to. She stands up and seizes control of the situation by suggesting that as he hired her precisely for her qualities as a manager, he cannot really turn around now and question her approach. This tactic is an attempt to make *him* responsible for *her* behavior. The Project Manager is trying to avoid responsibility for her actions and place responsibility for her conduct with the Sales Director. Then the Project Manager simply walks out of the room, leaving the Sales Director confused and lost for words.

The Third Instance: The Project Manager uses anger to try and persuade the Sales Director that he ought not to pursue his line of enquiry. She angrily suggests that someone in the office has spoken about her behind her back and demands to know who. She speaks in an outraged tone, portraying herself as the injured party and the victim of unfounded slander. Worse, she suggests that the Sales Director shouldn't be listening to gossip about her and should be saying 'well done' to someone who has done a sterling job for him in the past few weeks. Her strategy is to manipulate the Sales Director while also demanding that he tell her who said what *and* pat her on the back.

When he tries again, this time saying it is he who has concerns about the dip in morale in the team, she simply denies the validity of his observations. She tells him that his perceptions are wrong and puts forward an opposing point of view: that the team is not downhearted but is working hard at tasks she has assigned them. This ploy turns the fact that the team is demoralized into a matter of interpretation and leaves the Sales Director with nowhere to go. He cannot reveal who has said what because he has promised confidentiality to each of the four staff members who spoke with him previously that day. He does not want to risk alienating them by breaking his word. His own view about the demeanor of the team in the office is not one that is supported by the Project Manager. She claims that the conduct of the team members should be viewed in a very different light to his. There seems to be no point in arguing about who's right and who's wrong. From the Sales Director's point of view the meeting ends with no progress being made and with more questions raised than answered.

Confrontation: Conclusions

What conclusions can we come to about the action described above? Firstly, we can conclude that the Project Manager is a formidable foe indeed. Whichever way she plays it she is skilled at turning the tables on the Sales Director. She uses her well-developed tactics of obfuscating, blaming, scapegoating, denying the validity of his perceptions and projecting self-righteous anger at him to confuse him, change the point of the discussion, cloud the issues he wants to speak about with bogus ones and end the meeting prematurely, buying herself time and hoping to put him off the trail.

Secondly, we can also conclude that the Sales Director is going to have to use a much more resolute and skillful approach with the Project Manager if he is to get to the bottom of things quickly. Up until now he has assumed that he could have a constructive discussion with her about the issues – as he would with anyone else in the team about a performance issue he wants to raise. He now realizes that that isn't going to be the case, and that any attempt by him to open up the discussion he wants to have will be vigorously resisted by her. This is not an approach he has come up against before and it baffles him. Rather than trust him – as anyone else in the team would have done in a conversation with him about their performance issues – she treats him as if he is being completely unreasonable and very unfair toward her.

Thirdly, now that he has some firsthand experience of her trickery, he can be in no doubt that she is challenging in the extreme to deal with. Even forearmed with the testimony he secured earlier in the day from his four longest serving team members, he now realizes just how difficult it will be to pin her down. Arguing with her about perceptions isn't going to work. Neither is saying that he has concerns that he wants her to address. He will have to try again and this time with specific behavioral feedback based on his observations of her conduct around the office.

CONFRONTING A WORKPLACE BULLY

So how do you confront a workplace bully effectively? How do you avoid all the pitfalls that the Sales Director fell into? How do you keep the conversation clearly focused around the conduct of the bully and prevent it from degenerating into an unproductive and messy argument?

The starting point when confronting a workplace bully about their conduct is to provide them with *accurate, clear feedback on their behavior based on your observations of them* wherever possible. As their manager you should have more scope than most to observe them carrying out their day-to-day duties and you should be able to observe them interacting with their team and the people they target easily enough. You don't need to witness their worst excesses in order to provide them with effective feedback. You probably won't see these as they are likely to be carried out in secret, in one-to-one meetings. However, you do need to witness them doing something untoward first hand.

In addition to your first hand observations, you can also approach people who you suspect are being targeted by the workplace bully and ask them for specific behavioral examples of bullying. This is the approach taken by the Sales Director in the above example. Some people may be willing to provide you with information, others may not and even those who will talk to you might not want you to use what they have said. You will need to approach these interviews with tact, sensitivity and, if requested to do so by the people being targeted, complete confidentiality. However, the value to you of having conducted them is that you will know in your heart of hearts that the person you suspect of using bullying behavior has a track record of using abusive and coercive methods with a range of people at work. You can hold on to this fact alongside your own observations of them around the office.

Having assembled the feedback you want to present to the workplace bully how do you handle the meeting you need to have with them so that it is an effective confrontation of their behavior rather than the start of an escalation of the issues? Here are some ideas:

- The first thing you need to do is plan what you are going to say in detail and rehearse it. The benefit of taking this approach is that you will have your words off pat and won't be looking for them at the meeting. You can then use all of your energy in the meeting to respond to the obfuscating tactics the bully is likely to employ when confronted.
- Your strongest suit is to select one or two instances which you want to feed back to the bully. For each of them, make a direct link between the behavior you observed them using and the impact it had on the person they bullied. Then outline the way in which this behaviour has adversely affected your view of them and as well as outlining your expectations of their behaviour and performance from now on. This last point is very important. You are their manager and your view of them counts for something.
- Then proceed to outline what the continued use of these behaviors will mean for them and what view of them you will continue to hold if they don't cease using them.
- Then you can either end the meeting or ask them for a reaction to what you've said, whichever you see fit. At this point, you can expect them to create fog around the issues you have presented them with. If they do, you can let them finish and then, in a firm and level tone, reiterate your key points making it clear through your tone that you are committed to what you have just said.
- Then you can either ask for their reaction or end the meeting as you judge best.
- Finally, you need to be prepared to hold the confrontation sooner rather than later. Do it early. Don't wait. The longer you wait the more likely it will become that the bully will turn the tables on you.

They could tell you that they have been using their existing style for weeks or months without any complaints from you. They could ask you what has changed and leave you with the uncomfortable task of having to justify your decision to confront them. You might find it very difficult indeed to refocus the meeting around your preferred issue: that of holding them accountable for their bullying behaviour.

Your tone throughout the interview needs to be clear and firm. Your body language needs to convey confidence and clarity: sit upright, lean forward onto the desk, look engaged and keen to have the meeting, and make and keep level eye contact with your bullying team member. Body language like this will denote that you are prepared for this meeting, ready to have it and quite clear about what you are saying.

Don't vary the tone of your voice: keep it firm, clear and even. When your bullying colleague tries to deflect responsibility for their behavior elsewhere – on to you, on to the pressure they're under, on to their supposedly underperforming colleagues – don't fall for it: be prepared to reiterate your key points again and again in the same tone, giving the bully the clear message that you won't be bamboozled and you can see well enough what is actually going on.

WHY WILL THIS APPROACH SUCCEED?

What is it about this approach that makes it likely to succeed at calling a bully to account? Basically, it involves you holding the bully to responsible for their behavior, and it makes it difficult for them to wriggle out of it. This approach involves:

- You describing things they have said and done in clear, behavioral terms. They simply cannot deny a well put description of what they have said and done given to them by someone who heard what they said and saw what they did.
- You personally holding them accountable for the impact of their conduct on their colleagues. You are not speaking on behalf of someone else who's complained to you about them. You are speaking with them because you, their manager, have decided to having seen what you saw them do and heard what you heard them say.
- A clear demonstration of cause and effect which is compelling and hard to resist. By describing their behavior (the cause) and its result-ant consequences for them (the effect) in simple, straightforward language you present the bully with evidence of their wrongdoing *and its unpleasant ramifications for them*. This will make them think twice because you are clearly saying that they won't get away with

it. In other words you are outlining the consequences for the bully if they continue to use bullying behavior. This gives the bully a clear choice: continue to use abusive behavior and take the consequences or cease using it and avoid those unpleasant outcomes.

- You remaining in control of the interview despite the tactics that the bully will likely employ as they try to avoid responsibility for their actions.

Let's return to the action and see what happens next:

Example Three: Unmasked

The Sales Director has had enough. Having tried to speak with the Project Manager and failed to get her to engage with the issues, he decides to take another tack. He watches her around the office and after seeing two instances of her using an unnecessarily cutting tone with two of the team members her calls her into the meeting room for a chat.

He is already in the room when she arrives and, without getting up, he asks her to sit down. He leans forward, puts his hands together on the desk and makes level contact with the Project Manager. Then he begins to speak in a level, firm tone maintaining eye contact with her all the time. He tells her that he has been observing her around the office and he wants to feed back one or two things to her. Without pausing for breath he tells her that he observed her that afternoon using a cutting and unpleasant tone with two members of staff and that he saw the two people flinch at their desks and go white in the face when being addressed that way.

At this point the Project Manager tries to interrupt but the Sales Director holds up the flat of his hand toward her and tells her and he is speaking. He then informs her that his view of her has been affected by these two incidents, and that it is his view that there are plenty of other incidents – of perhaps a worse and more unpleasant nature – that he could cite as well. He tells her, as she sits visibly discomforted in her seat, that he will not tolerate the use of coercive behavior by a manager in his team. He tells her that if she uses coercive methods with any member of the team she will have to answer to him. He tells her that her use of veiled or outright aggression must cease and that he will be looking from that point on for evidence that it has ceased. He pauses for effect and then tells her that he suspects that the downbeat and dejected atmosphere in the team is a direct consequence of her aggressive methods of handling people and that she needs to find a new, more productive and more effective way of managing the team. He asks her if she has anything to say.

There are a number of ways in which the Project Manager could respond to this question. Let's examine some of her options:

- The Project Manager could tell the Sales Director that he is mistaken and that what he heard her say wasn't evidence of aggression but was evidence of her commitment to high quality work. She could suggest that her reaction was one of disappointment at seeing below par work, especially as she had already spoken to the two team members about the standard she wanted to see beforehand. But she runs a significant risk if she does this: firstly, the Sales Director could ask to see the work in question and even a cursory examination of it would reveal it wasn't that substandard; secondly, she risks overplaying her hand if she tries to suggest that the Sales Director's perceptions are at fault in a situation he has already said he holds her accountable for.
- The Project Manager could use anger to deny the allegations against her. This is risky too: she would be exhibiting exactly the type of behavior the Sales Director has just said he doesn't want to see her using.
- The Project Manager could say that she finds the culture of the team too slow and lacking in pace and that she's used to working with more upbeat, decisive and independent people. This is also risky because, now that he's on the ball, the Sales Director might suggest that it, if that's the case, then perhaps his team is not the right place for her to work.
- The Project Manager could promise that the two instances of aggression witnessed by the Sales Director will be one-offs and won't happen again. She could then end the interview and return to her desk, hoping that, after a few days, he'll forget about it and she can continue to bully her team members in peace and behind his back. Assuming that she wants to continue to bully her team members this approach could work for her. But then she can't know for sure exactly how committed the Sales Director is to his verbal promise that she'll have to account to him if she steps out of line again. She decides, on balance, that the best line to take is to tell the Sales Director that, yes, she has been 'on edge' over the past few days and won't let her commitment to high-quality work spill over into aggression again.

Unmasked: Conclusions

What conclusions can we draw based on the action described above? Firstly, we can say that the resolve and determination demonstrated by the Sales Director when confronting the Project Manager have had an impact on her. She now knows that he isn't the soft touch she initially thought him to be and she can see clearly that he means what he says – at least for this interview. But she wonders to what extent he will be committed to his resolute words when the rubber hits the road and he is snowed under with work and traveling all over the country again. She thinks her cards have been marked for now, but doesn't think it is necessary the end of the road for her bullying behavior.

Secondly, we can conclude that what the Sales Director does after this meeting is crucial. He cannot afford to come across as halfhearted in his assertion that he wants to see sustained behavior change from his Project Manager; nor can he afford to spend too much time out of the office, time during which the Project Manager could easily go back to her old ways. He needs to follow up this meeting with other meetings at which he gives her feedback on her behavior and his assessment of her conduct around the office. He needs to continue to test the temperature in the team, and speak to his four longest-serving team members about the Project Manager's behaviour with them. He needs to realize that his usual trusting style of management isn't going to be effective with the Project Manager, and that he has to be on his toes with her from this moment onward. Basically, he needs to decide whether or not he is prepared to work with her for the long term, given the time commitment he is likely to have to make to managing her.

Thirdly, we don't know whether the Project Manager is capable of altering her approach to handling the team members she is responsible for managing. She isn't good with people and it is possible that, without sustained managerial-skills development, she won't know how to alter her approach sufficiently to come up to the Sales Director's expectations. He also needs to determine whether or not he wants to invest in her development. Assuming he does, it is possible that she won't see the need or would be offended by the suggestion that she needs to learn new people-handling skills. There is a lot for the Sales Director to ponder now that he has confronted the Project Manager and only time will tell how much progress he will ultimately make with her – and how much commitment he has to the challenge of working with her.

Confronting a Workplace Bully: Key Lessons

Failing to confront the fact that you might have a workplace bully in your team is often the path of least resistance and can seem, amid high workloads and the pressure of working life, the easiest option. But it isn't in the long run. Failing to confront a workplace bully will send a clear message to your team members that, by your decision not to act, you are condoning the bullying. You may not be authorizing it or actively cooperating with it, but you are allowing it to happen when you could act to prevent it.

Managers who don't act against workplace bullying once they know it is happening, enable it to continue. And they often find that their initial reluctance to confront the bully and require them to stop bullying creates further issues in their team down the road, issues which affect team performance, output and morale. These issues could include team members:

- Feeling resentful and angry toward their employer for not protecting them from an abusive situation.
- Doing just enough at work and putting their energy and commitment into other areas of their lives, believing that their welfare isn't important to their manager.
- Taking short or long term sick leave to cope with the stress they experience as a result of being bullied at work.
- Performing at increasingly low levels as their energy and enthusiasm for their jobs are sapped by the bullying they are subject to.
- Deciding to leave the team and seek employment elsewhere, leaving you with the task and expense of replacing them.
- Taking legal action against their employer – and implicating you – for failing to prevent bullying at work.

SUMMARY AND NEXT CHAPTER

This chapter has examined the issues facing a manager who realizes that they might have a workplace bully in their team. The chapter has illustrated the situation from the point of view of team members who are too afraid to spill the beans; from the point of view of the workplace bully who doesn't want to participate in a conversation with their manager about their behavior and from the point of view of the manager who decides that they must get to the bottom of it all.

This chapter has:

- Highlighted a series of pitfalls that managers can inadvertently fall into when they set about gathering evidence of workplace bullying in order to confront the bully.
- Illustrated some of the strategies that a bullying team member could use to avoid responsibility for their actions and deflect it elsewhere.

- Suggested a protocol that you might like to employ when you do confront someone you think guilty of consistently using bullying behavior at work.

The next chapter will focus on the issues facing family and friends of someone subject to workplace bullying. It will highlight how the target of workplace bullying can start to behave differently at home and in social situations, and will describe steps that their friends and families can take to support them effectively through their experience of being bullied at work.

CHAPTER 7

The Role of Friends and Family Members
Supporting Someone You Know Through an Experience of Workplace Bullying

Your friend or family member is going through a hard time at work. They are coming home – or meeting you socially – looking down and low. They are not their usual selves. They might seem drained and listless – or angry and sullen – but, however they show it, clearly all is not well with them. They might not feel like talking or taking part in their regular hobbies and pastimes. They might not have much energy or interest to contribute to the things you normally talk about and do together. They might or might not have come to the conclusions that their work difficulties constitute 'an experience of workplace bullying' but, whichever way you look at it, they are going through a tough time.

This chapter is for those of you who identify with the fact that your friend or family member is going through the mill at work, and realize that their challenges go well beyond common workplace difficulties like having too much to do or working for an unsupportive boss. It is written for those of you who:

- Think that your friend or family member is being bullied and want to know more about what they might be experiencing from their point of view.
- Want to understand how their experiences are likely to be affecting them mentally and behaviorally.
- Want some ideas about how best to support them through this difficult time.

The objectives of this chapter are to:

- Describe some of your friend or family member's experiences from the inside out.

- Highlight some of the reasons why your friend or family member might pull away from social contact while being subject to workplace bullying.
- Identify the ways in which your support can make a positive contribution to them coping with their experience of workplace bullying.
- Suggest some practical things you could do to provide them with effective support.

A CHANGE IN BEHAVIOR

Many people who become subject to bullying at work start to behave differently outside the workplace. They just don't do things the way they normally would. They find it difficult to maintain their usual level of enthusiasm and interest in their hobbies, social activities and pastimes. They often leave work exhausted from having, as they see it, to fight for their survival during the day and don't have the level of energy or commitment that they would normally have to give to their friends and family members. They don't want to be a burden, might not find it easy to confide in anyone but would benefit from support.

They may or may not find that their friends and family members are equipped to listen to them and help them in ways they find supportive. Consider the following examples:

- A team leader in a humanitarian organization is subject to constant workplace bullying by a peer who, sadly, has a good relationship with the CEO. The team leader worries that her friends and family will reduce her experiences of workplace bullying to 'difficulties at work', and is concerned that, if she speaks with them about the reality of the behavior to which she is subject, they will say: 'we all have difficult people to deal with at work' and leave it at that. She doesn't think they will really be equipped to hear just how personally damaging her peer's conduct toward her is, and won't appreciate the effect of having it unknowingly enabled by the CEO. So she doesn't confide in anyone and struggles on alone, feeling ashamed at not being able to cope as effectively as she used to.
- A teacher is subject to constant workplace bullying by the head of the school where he works. He goes home everyday and tells his supportive partner what has happened. He often tells his friends, in regular phone calls, what has been going on during the day. His friends and family members are all astonished at what is going on and often start their conversations with him with the words 'what has he done now?' They react incredulously to his descriptions of

his boss's behavior. Their reactions reinforce the teacher's growing belief that he is subject to workplace bullying and they validate his gut instinct that he is being singled out for a prolonged and unjustified attack. Their support proves invaluable in helping him cope. It helps him put what is happening to him at work into some sort of perspective each evening. He is able to distance himself from the bullying somewhat and isn't completely engulfed by it. He thinks that, without their support, he would 'crack up'.

- A management consultant is subject to constant workplace bullying by her manager. Living a long way away from her family she turns to her local friends for support. She particularly wants to hear their perspective on what is happening to her and so bounces off them some of the actions and behaviors which her manager is subjecting her to. Her friends listen for a while but are not very interested in what is happening to her or what it means to her. They are not able to empathize with her situation and, not being that sympathetic either, they quickly lose interest in it. They suggest that she do something practical like go on a scuba diving holiday. She thinks they are trivializing what she is experiencing and she starts to spend less time with them. This approach means that she protects herself from the disappointment of having unsupportive friends at a time of crisis in her life, but it also leaves her socially isolated which she feels keenly.

- A university IT manager is subject to constant workplace bullying by her manager and turns to her partner for help. Her partner is very much affected by what she is going through at work and the IT manager worries about the impact that her experiences are having on him. By the time her manager is asked to leave the university ten months later she is convinced that her partner has suffered as much as her – if not more.

- A government worker is subject to constant workplace bullying by his key peer. He is buoyed to realize that his team members and his other peers are very aware of what he is going through. They encourage him, telling him to 'keep going' and 'not be put off' by the behavior to which he is subject. They seem to understand the impact the individual instances of bullying that they witness have on him and are able to empathize with the cumulative effect of behavior which he experiences as personally punishing and aimed solely at him. He realizes that, without their support, he wouldn't be able to cope. He thinks that, without their help and their perspective on his experiences, he might quickly come to believe that what is happening to him is either his own fault or is due to him being less competent at his job than he thinks he is.

These examples illustrate a range of reactions that friends and family members can have when someone they know is subject to workplace bullying. They demonstrate just how vital an effective source of support can be for someone subject to workplace bullying. Why does it matter so much?

THE CHALLENGE OF WORKPLACE BULLYING

Workplace bullying causes enormous pressures and stresses to be placed upon the people subject to it. It means that they have to adjust to and deal with unwarranted, relentless personal attacks from workplace contacts whom they cannot avoid encountering. It means that they have to live with the day-to-day reality that they might:

- Not feel safe at work.
- Not know how to defend themselves against the bullying they are experiencing.
- Not get any effective support from their employers.
- Work for managers who don't think it's their job to do anything about the bullying they are subject to.
- Not know how to change the situation they are in.
- Not have the energy or self-belief to get out of the situation by looking for another job.
- Work for employers who *do* care about what is happening to them but are ineffective at preventing the bullying from reoccurring.

In addition to this, even though they are experiencing workplace bullying, every employee still needs to perform in their role. They need to continue to meet their workplace targets and perform satisfactorily in their roles, just as they did before they became subject to workplace bullying. They need to find the energy and mental capacity to:

- Carry out their normal workplace duties.
- Input to meetings.
- Think.
- Make decisions.
- Give opinions.
- Keep their workplace commitments.
- Maintain their workplace relationships.

Then they need to go home, contribute to their home-based relationships and find some ways of recovering and recharging their batteries before doing it all again the next day, and the day after that, and the day after that. They need to get on with things while also having to deal with the constant assaults upon their well-being.

REACTIONS TO WORKPLACE BULLYING

So how is your friend or family member likely to be reacting to the bullying they are subject to? Different people react to workplace bullying in different ways based on their disposition and coping strategies. Some people turn their anger in on themselves and become depressed. Others withdraw and spend more time alone. Some people become sullen and demanding. Still others start to use greater aggression with their colleagues even if they'd never have thought of doing so under normal circumstances.

Consider the following examples:

- A quality conscious, quiet but determined team leader is subject to workplace bullying from his arrogant and more aggressive boss. In order to cope with the bullying he is experiencing the team leader starts booking a meeting room for 3–4 hours a day to get away from his manager, time which takes him away from his team and makes it difficult for them to get his input to important or urgent items. He becomes negative and pessimistic, quicker to blame his team for errors and inconsistencies in their work and resistant to requests for help from coworkers from other teams. He realizes that he is not behaving as he normally would and doesn't like the changes he experiences in himself, but he is unable to do anything about it. Too much of his energy and internal resources are tied up in trying to cope with his bullying boss.
- An outgoing and ebullient project manager is subject to workplace bullying by her jealous and threatened manager. In order to cope with the bullying she is experiencing the project manager starts jogging before and after work often arriving later than she normally would. She prioritizes her work more ruthlessly, and begins delegating tasks that she really should attend to herself but finds she doesn't want to do anymore. She starts to take long lunches, often returning late to her office. She develops a degree of passive-aggression toward her colleagues, worries about the quality of her team's work but doesn't monitor its outputs and withdraws from workplace social activities. She starts to feel angry with herself for not being as bubbly as she used to be and realizes that she is 'losing herself'. But she doesn't

know how to alter her behavior back to what it used to be and struggles on feeling as if she is only 'half the person she used to be'.

- A calm and methodical assistant director is subject to workplace bullying by her envious peer. The assistant director starts to talk with her team colleagues at great length before feeling able to make a decision. She spends more time alone in her office with the door closed in order to regain control of her feelings, and consequently begins to lose touch with her team's work. She struggles to identify and confront growing problems in her team – something that she was both able and eager to tackle before she became the target of a workplace bully. She becomes more and more inflexible and starts to use a dominating and authoritarian approach with her team members. At other times she withdraws into her office with the door closed and worries about her dwindling reputation. She can herself swinging from aggression to inactivity but doesn't know how to arrest the trend and regain the stability and balance that marked her approach to her work before she was bullied.
- A logical, decisive and interpersonally warm technologist is subject to workplace bullying by his manager. Feeling that he is losing control of his own emotions he begins to adopt an overly rigid and controlling approach with his team. He becomes more directive and more insensitive, displaying a degree of coldness around the office that surprises his colleagues. He reacts with temper and impatience to perfectly reasonable questions from his team members and becomes both inefficient and unproductive in his own work. Unable to let his guard down in the office and talk about the difficulties he is experiencing he goes home after work and confides in his partner. He talks at length about how he isn't as resourceful or likeable as he used to be. He is unable to understand his own reaction to his experiences or to 'click back' into working the way he used to do. He begins to see himself as the problem – not the experience of workplace bullying he is subject to.

These examples describe a range of visible, behavioral changes to their normal way of doing things that people being bullied at work might make. Let's now look at a range of other changes, more internal, that people subject to workplace bullying might also resort to as they look for ways to handle the situation they are in.

THINKING DIFFERENT THOUGHTS

Many of the changes that people subject to workplace bullying make are internal and therefore, by and large, hidden. Some people who are being bullied start to think differently about themselves and others. They might start to think that they are less capable than they thought they were, doubting themselves in ways they wouldn't have done before they were bullied. They might start to think that they deserve the treatment they are getting or think that it's somehow their fault and that they caused it to happen. They might start to believe some of the things being said about them by the person bullying them: that they are weak or inadequate or incompetent or aren't good enough or don't fit in.

As well as affecting their self-image an experience of workplace bullying can also result in those subject to it starting to question areas of their lives which up until that point, they wouldn't have doubted. They might start to think that they are not as close to their friends or family members as they thought they were. They might start to see a job which they used to enjoy – and an employer whom they previously thought of as good to work for – in less positive terms.

Consider the following example:

- A newly qualified teacher joins her first school and is keen to impress. Her class is in a single storey cabin positioned away from the main building and she initially finds it difficult to make contact with the other teachers at break times and during the lunch hour. From day one she feels somewhat isolated professionally so, when she is offered the opportunity to be mentored by the most established teacher at school, she jumps at the chance and into an experience of workplace bullying. The more experienced teacher undermines her new colleague from the off, questioning her judgement and verbalizing her distrust of the more junior teacher's instincts. The impact of being repeatedly treated as if she is incompetent and likely to make mistakes leaves the new teacher, over time, *feeling* both incompetent and likely to make mistakes. She starts to doubt her own intuitions. She begins double-checking that she has in fact completed the tasks she has just completed. She goes back over her written work and reads it again to make sure that she does agree with what she's just written. She finds it hard to trust herself and rarely acts on her own instincts. In a misguided attempt to avoid making errors which will lead to another instance of bullying, she begins trying to think everything through logically and rationally, instead of just doing what she wants to do. Her mind constantly whirrs, looking for an explanation about how she could have become so unable to trust herself in a profession she was so looking forward to. She can't rest at home and is tired all the time. She doesn't sleep well and often wakes up feeling fatigued. Over time, she begins to see herself as ill suited to teaching, something she has always wanted to do, and considers moving into another field instead. She expends so much energy using adapted behavior – thinking things through, double-checking her work, preventing herself from acting on her instincts – that she becomes depleted and drained, and has less and less energy or enthusiasm to give to the children in her care. In the absence of any effective source of support inside or outside school, she doesn't recognize that the flak she's getting from the more established teacher is both unjustified and pejorative. She absorbs it and comes to see herself as ineffectual and deficient as a teacher, rather than perceive her experiences as being symptomatic of sustained workplace bullying.

One of the main coping strategies that people who are being bullied at work use is adapting their behavior. In order to be ready for an encounter with the person bullying them – and to be able to deal with the consequences for them of that encounter – people subject to workplace bullying often alter their usual approach. They do this because they:

- Hope that by altering *their* way of doing things they will stand some chance of influencing the bully to cease using destructive behavior.
- Come to believe that the 'problem' lies with them rather than the behavior to which they are subject so they try and alter their own behavior to correct the problem and 'get it right'.

Unfortunately, adapting their behavior often results in the person becoming even more depleted as they repeatedly use an unnatural, adapted approach instead of their more natural, spontaneous one. It can also mean that the quality of their work suffers as they cease playing to their strengths and start to use less practiced and less skilled ways of doing things.

USING ADAPTED BEHAVIOR

So how much adaptation does someone subject to workplace bullying typically make? The degree of adaptation that anyone person will feel the need to make will vary from person to person and from situation to situation. But it is likely that, however much or however little a person feels the need to use adapted behavior, doing so will constitute a very real drain on their energy reserves especially if they feel the need to maintain adapted behavior for any length of time.

Consider the following example:

■ An assertive and confident operations manager becomes subject to workplace bullying. She hasn't been treated in this way before and is completely taken by surprise by her manager's behavior toward her. Her manager bullies her in private and in public and, while the operations manager is quite used to holding her own in tough verbal exchanges at work, she is quite unprepared for the degree of personalized assault that she experiences from her manager. In order to try and deal with her boss's behavior she adopts a more vigorous and brusque demeanor around the office. She speaks more sharply, provides less rationale and background before presenting her point of view and becomes much more goal orientated in her dealings with her boss. Using the adapted approach drains her because it isn't natural and results in her being less effective at her job because it doesn't play to her characteristic strengths. She makes less effective decisions, uses her time less well and fails to respond to her team's queries with her characteristic whole-hearted enthusiasm. Her manager, however, barely notices her change of approach and, being someone largely focused on her own agenda, continues to use bullying behavior as and when she feels like it.

Many people subject to bullying do find a way through their experience. They cope and come out on the other side. However, having a supportive friend or family member can enable them to handle the experience more effectively, can result in less strain being placed on their beleaguered systems and, in some instances, can make all the difference.

So what role could you, as a friend or family member, play in helping support them during their experience of workplace bullying?

PROVIDING EFFECTIVE SUPPORT

As a friend or family member you can play a valuable role in supporting someone you know through their experience of workplace bullying. Let's take a look at the different ways in which you can help them:

■ Many people subject to workplace bullying find it hard to acknowledge or express just how angry they are at being bullied. Often your friend or family member will be angry with several people: the bully themselves as well as other people who they think have enabled the bullying, people such as their senior managers who turn a blindeye or previous people who've been bullied by the same person and didn't speak up about it. It is vital that your friend or family member finds a safe place to express their anger. Otherwise they run the risk of turning their anger in on themselves and becoming vulnerable to depression.

- People who are being bullied at work need somewhere where they can tell their story and gain some sort of perspective on what is happening to them. Simply by listening to their story and reacting as you normally would to what you hear can help them realize that what is happening to them is not justified. Many people subject to workplace bullying need to have external validation of their feelings, especially when the bullying they receive is out of the blue or from someone with whom they had previously had a positive working relationship. As a friend or family member your reactions of astonishment and anger or amazement at the instances described to you can be very helpful – even liberating – to someone trying to work out whether or not what they are experiencing is out of the norm and whether or not it constitutes workplace bullying.

- Knowing that they have somewhere to go after work where they can speak about what is happening to them during the day can, in and of itself, help someone subject to workplace bullying cope better with the experience. They know that they will be able to explore what has happened to them that day and talk about what it means to them. In doing so they will hopefully hear another person's view on their situation and be able to put what is happening to them into some sort of perspective. They know that they will be heard by someone supportive and interested and this will give them courage.

- Listening to your ideas and suggestions about how you'd react if you were in their shoes can provide your friend or family member with additional strategies and tactics to employ back at work which might enable them to better handle their assailant. People who are being bullied at work and who are struggling to handle the situation can end up using the same ineffective behavior over and over again in successive abusive situations. Listening to how you would react should you be treated as they are being treated, can help your friend or family member to identify different ways to handle bullying behavior the next time they encounter it – ways which might prove more effective than their current approaches and which might enable them to better protect themselves and challenge the bullying dynamic.

- Depending on how used to speaking about their thoughts and feelings they may be, your friend or family member might find it helpful simply to have you reflect back to them what they are saying to you about their experiences. Some people are affected so deeply by their experiences of workplace bullying that they cannot put into words what it means to them. They don't have a language with which to articulate the loss of control or powerlessness or the levels of distress which they feel and, unable to communicate what their experiences mean to them, they can quickly feel isolated and alone. Being able to speak about how upset they are can be very helpful for your friend or family member should they begin to feel disconnected and alone.

■ Finally, being bullied can leave many people feeling ashamed. Being able to talk to a friend or family member and find that they still value and care for them can be important in helping someone subject to workplace bullying retain some self-esteem and self-confidence in an abusive situation.

SEEKING PROFESSIONAL HELP

All that said, many people subject to workplace bullying also need skilled, professional help to enable them to assimilate what has happened to them and recover from it. If your friend or family member hasn't already taken this step you can play a role in:

■ Deciding when you think this point has been reached.
■ Encouraging your friend or family member to seek the services of a professional skilled at helping people who've been bullied at work.
■ Suggesting that your friend or family member contact their GP should they need medical support.

However, it's not your job to bite off more than you can chew. If you think you can't cope with the level of distress being demonstrated by your friend or family member don't simply walk away. Stay with them and encourage them to find professional help. There are more and more sources of help available for people being bullied at work. The last chapter of this book entitled References, Websites and Further Reading will point you in the right direction.

PRACTICAL THINGS YOU CAN DO TO HELP

Assuming that you have decided that you want to help your friend or family member through their experience of workplace bullying, the most basic and helpful things you can do are to:

■ Listen to them as they describe what is happening at work and how it is affecting them.

- Encourage them to remain part of their social and family circles, taking part in their normal round of hobbies and pastimes, even if on a reduced scale.

Here are some other simple ideas that will be beneficial too:

- *Write Down the Day's Experiences*: Ask your friend or family member to write down a headline or a phrase for each of the day's upsetting bullying events. Ask them to generate one headline or phrase for every bullying incident that happened that day, including big incidents and smaller ones. If they have access to a flipchart they could do this exercise on the flipchart; if not, they could write it down on paper. Each evening, or every few days, talk through the incidents one by one, asking them what the incident means to them, what they feel (or think) about the incident and what conclusions they've come to about themselves as a result of it. Write this information down next to the relevant headline or phrase. You can then make it your role to challenge any false conclusions or incorrect assumptions that your friend or family member is making about themselves as a result of their experiences on that day. For instance, if your friend or family member is starting to tell themselves that they're not as good at their job as they thought they were, you can tell them that that's not true and point to some validation that you know about: maybe their last appraisal rating or the fact that they recently won a new contract for their employer or are due for promotion. Doing this will help your friend or family member to objectify what has happened to them that day and gain some emotional distance from the events. It will also enable them to review what they've written and keep the truth about their competence and their personal qualities in mind rather than being engulfed by the bully's perceptions of them.
- *Create Space for Them:* There are many ways to do this and even an extra half hour to themselves on an evening or during the weekend will help your friend or family member have some time to reflect and recharge their batteries before going back to work. You could create this space for them by doing the cooking or the weekly shopping in their stead, walking their dog for them, doing their housework or taking their children out for the afternoon so they can have some time to themselves.
- *Organize Treats:* Again there are many possibilities here but the point is to time a treat for when your friend or family member has the physical and mental capacity to enjoy it, so that it doesn't

become something else they have to do. You could arrange something they'd enjoy that will take them out of themselves: perhaps a visit to the theater or ballet; a walk along the coast; an afternoon at a sports event; a weekend away in a country cottage; a meal out; an evening at a country pub; or a family visit to a theme park, the zoo or the coast.

There are many creative ways you could think of to help keep your friend or family member connected to and playing a part in the 'normal' world outside their workplace. You'll find your own way. The important thing to bear in mind is that your friend or family member may well be stretched to the limit coping with their experiences at work and the time they spend outside work is vital to their capacity to cope effectively with their ongoing workplace challenges. Handling their experience effectively does fall to them and remains their responsibility, but you can play a key role in supporting them through it.

SUMMARY AND NEXT CHAPTER

This chapter has examined the issue of workplace bullying from the point of view of friends or family members of people experiencing workplace bullying.

This chapter has:

■ Described a range of behavioral and internal adaptations that your friend or family member might use to help them cope with the bullying.
■ Examined some of the potential consequences for them of employing these coping strategies.
■ Suggested ways in which, as their friend or family member, you can provide vital support and practical assistance to them during their experience of workplace bullying.
■ Encouraged you to help your friend or family member seek professional support should they need it and not be taking those steps themselves.

The following chapter changes tack and is the major case study in the book. The case study gives you an opportunity to read the action, apply the lessons from the first seven chapters of the book to the scenario and gain knowledge of further interpersonal tactics and skills that can be helpful to you should you become subject to workplace bullying. The action follows the fate of an employee of a company who is subject to workplace bullying and describes how her senior manager reacts to the knowledge that one of his team leaders is consistently using bullying behavior at work.

CHAPTER 8

A Cautionary Tale
A Case Study

The following case study is an opportunity for you to analyze and determine how to respond to an evolving campaign of workplace bullying. The case study is set in a fictional soft drinks manufacturer and focuses primarily on the relationships between a newly appointed Customer Services Manager, her boss the Marketing Manager and her boss the Sales Director.

As you read on you will see that the case study is presented in portions. Following each section of the case study you will find questions to be answered which give you an opportunity to delveinto the action and analyze the deeper dynamics at play between the main protagonists. You can jot down your answers to these questions in the space following each one, and can subsequently compare your answers to those you will find at the end of the chapter.

RETURNING TO WORK

A woman returner to the job market decides to apply for a role in the customer services department of a soft drinks manufacturer. Previous to taking time off to devote to her children, she used to work in training and development and in HR roles. She believes that these experiences have equipped her with experience and skills at handling people, and she thinks that she will be able to run the team of nine people at the drinks manufacturer's Head Office which is eight miles from her home. After a lengthy interview and selection process she is delighted to be offered the role and accepts the position.

The soft drinks manufacturer sells everything from bottled water to cartons of fruit juice, and from canned carbonated drinks to nonalcoholic designer bottled drinks. It receives thousands of Internet enquiries and orders each day from around the world, as well as doing business with hundreds of worldwide retail outlets such as hotels, shops, restaurants, pubs, clubs and catering companies. The woman returner's team handles customer queries via the company's website and by letter, fax, e-mail and telephone. The team has developed a reputation for being both speedy and effective at handling the range of queries, complaints, questions and requests for after-sales services which come its way.

THE NEW ROLE

The new Customer Services Manager reports to the Marketing Manager whom she first meets during the selection process. During the final selection meeting the Marketing Manager tells the candidates that she reports to the Sales Director and that the Sales Director reports to the Chief Executive Officer. The Customer Services Manager forms the view that her new manager might be tricky to deal with, being both distant and detached as well as status conscious.

The customer services team sits at a bank of computers arranged around a square of inward-facing desks. Their manager sits at her computer at one end of the square. The Marketing Manager has a glass-panelled office in the same large first floor office space that houses the customer services team. Other teams housed in the same space include the accounts team, the web team and the logistics team who handle the delivery side of the Internet-based sales business. The company's four Directors and its CEO have offices on the second floor.

From day one the Customer Services Manager is uncomfortable in her job.

Initially she cannot quite put her finger on what is wrong. She senses rather than knows that something is amiss, but doesn't have any firm evidence to point to. She cannot figure out what is at the bottom of her intuition that all is not well in the office. She tells herself not to worry and that she is simply getting used to being back at work after devoting time to her children – but her disquiet doesn't go away. After a particularly trying third day in which several issues flare up simultaneously, the Marketing Manager calls the new Customer Services Manager to her office at 4 p.m.

The Marketing Manager tells the Customer Services Manager that she is glad of the opportunity to catch up with her and find out how her time with the company is going. The Customer Services Manager says it's going well from her point of view and that she's finding her feet again after several years away from the workplace. The Marketing Manager tells her that she's sure the two of them 'will get along fine' and that she thinks that 'there is a clear meeting of minds' between the two of them. She then ends the meeting sharply but politely enough and the Customer Services Manager returns to her team feeling uncertain about what these two comments might mean.

Questions For You To Answer: Set One

Thinking about the action from the point of view of the Customer Services Manager answer the following three questions:

- Had she decided to respond to it at the time, how would you advise the Customer Services Manager to reply to the Marketing Manager's comment that the two of them 'will get along fine'?

- Had she decided to respond at the time, how would you advise the Customer Services Manager to reply to her boss's subsequent comment that 'there is a clear meeting of minds' between the two of them?

- What interpretation do you form about the Marketing Manager's motivation for saying these two things?

CHARACTER CAMEO ONE: THE MARKETING MANAGER

The Marketing Manager is 49. She is superficially warm and hospitable but is actually quite a cool character underneath. She has worked for the soft drinks manufacturer for ten years. The Marketing Manager doesn't really like people. She lacks the easy ability to build rapport with others which she envies in some of her colleagues. She is slightly superior in her demeanor, being both politically minded and status conscious. When the previous Customer Services Manager resigned, her preference was not to employ a replacement but to take the customer services team directly under her control. She was refused permission to do this by the Sales Director and the CEO and the company advertised for a new Customer Services Manager instead.

The Marketing Manager is reasonably imaginative in her approach to marketing the extensive range of soft drinks manufactured by the company, but secretly knows that the excellent reputation of the firm for delivery and after-sales service accounts for its repeat business much more so than her own marketing vision or acumen.

The Marketing Manager is by nature both skeptical and questioning. She is known for her critical and blunt treatment of what she sees as 'sloppy work' or 'avoidable errors'. She can be pressuring with her staff, especially after an interview with the CEO, whom she finds prickly and awkward to deal with. She is quite resentful of her own boss the Sales Director, and is jealous of his apparently close relationship with the CEO. She goes for a drink with the Sales Director twice a month to keep her ear to the ground as she is convinced that the CEO tells him information that he doesn't tell her and which she'd like to hear about.

The Marketing Manager doesn't mix well with anyone at workplace social events, preferring to adopt the role of moving around different groups of employees checking that everyone has sufficient to eat and drink. This role enables her to reinforce her authority as, as she sees it, the most influential woman in the company and the unofficial hostess for the evening.

A POSITIVE IMPRESSION

Over the next two weeks the Customer Services Manager has two conversations with the Sales Director. In each case the Sales Director seeks her out to ask her opinion about the frequency and content of after-sales queries. The Customer Services Manager has the information at her fingertips and impresses the Sales Director with her knowledge and speed of response. He forms the view that she appears on top of her job and comments favorably to the Marketing Manager about the performance to date of the new Customer Services Manager.

SLOPPY TIMEKEEPING?

The soft drinks manufacturer uses a flexitime system which allows its employees to arrive at a time that suits them between 7.30 a.m. and 9.30 a.m. The Customer Services Manager is in the habit of taking her two small children to school before coming to work. She usually arrives before a quarter past nine. However, on a Monday and Tuesday during the second week of her employment, roadworks cause her to arrive closer to 9.30 a.m. than she usually would.

On Wednesday morning she arrives to find an e-mail from her boss which says 'you should be at your desk by 9 a.m.'. The Customer Services Manager is taken aback and replies with an e-mail of her own. In it she tells the Marketing Manager that she is contractually allowed to arrive by 9.30 a.m. and that she has only been arriving after 9.15 a.m. recently due to roadworks. Later that day her manager sends her a reply which says 'that's ok – and I do realize that you stay late too'.

Questions For You To Answer: Set Two

Answer the following two questions which examine the issues surrounding the e-mail which the Marketing Manager sends to the Customer Services Manager criticizing her timekeeping:

■ The Customer Services Manager responds to her manager's e-mail with an e-mail of her own. But she doesn't go and talk the issue through with the Marketing Manager. What would have been the potential benefits to her of talking the issue through face-to-face?

■ Even though the Marketing Manager partially retracts her initial e-mail by acknowledging that the Customer Services Manager does stay late, she is still clearly irritated at something. What could account for her need to pick her team leader up on her timekeeping which, on the face of it, isn't poor?

INTENSE JOB

The Customer Services Manager enjoys her role but finds it a very intense one indeed. Her team of nine are good with difficult customers but regularly need input and advice from her. As well as managing the team, making sure that it reaches its response time targets and personally handling complaints from larger customers, she also finds herself increasingly asked to join planned and impromptu meetings by the Sales Director. She is pleased that he seems to value her opinion but also finds herself pulled in several directions at once, with too much to do and without anyone to turn to.

Her own manager isn't supportive, only gives her limited time and does so with obvious reluctance. When she does agree to a meeting she often continues to tap away at her computer while the Customer Services Manager speaks to her. The Marketing Manager makes it clear that she has much more pressing and important matters to attend to than listening to the Customer Services Manager and pressurizes the team leader into finishing the meeting before she wants to because she 'is busy'.

After three weeks, the Marketing Manager decides to handover responsibility for a new Customer Audit to the Customer Services Manager. The Audit will involve collecting data from small, medium and large customers from questionnaires designed to help the soft drinks manufacturer refine and improve its offer to customers. The Customer Services Manager worries that she simply won't have time to do the work properly but dares not confide her anxiety in her manager. She determines to do the best she can and mentions to the Sales Director, with whom she is developing a cordial relationship, that she is very busy at the moment.

CHARACTER CAMEO TWO: THE SALES DIRECTOR

The Sales Director is 52. He is an intelligent, industrious, manipulative and controlling character who has worked for the soft drinks manufacturer for 14 years. He is very aware of his own authority in the organization and doesn't react well to anyone who disagrees with him in public. He frequently says that he likes robust debate and welcomes contrary opinions from his people at meetings. But, whenever anyone does volunteer an opposing point of view, he is quick to talk them down making clear his preference for his input over theirs, and doing so with sufficient energy that they think twice before giving voice to their opposing views again in public.

The Sales Director is decisive, factual and logical. He is a deep thinker but is not that good at giving information to other people about the thought processes he has gone through prior to arriving at a decision. His decisions are usually delivered with a finality that precludes debate and, in the absence of too many clues about the mental route he has taken to arrive at them, can appear a bit arbitrary and, to more junior staff, somewhat intimidating.

However, he is an effective sales director, and is good at generating and sustaining revenue streams for the soft drinks company. He is also effective at managing the perceptions of the CEO quite carefully. On the one hand he is careful to shield him from anything that is going wrong or has already gone wrong, tending to give him good news rather than bad. On the other hand he is keen to agree in public with the CEO while, sometimes, disagreeing vehemently with him in private.

During these disputes he forcibly tells the CEO that he is 'forgetful' and 'off the pace' while also providing him with a pre-thought out plan of action to address whatever issue they are discussing; suggestions with which the CEO might initially disagree but which he adopts in the end. The Sales Director also writes the business plans and interim summaries that the CEO publishes to the company and claims as his own. It is the Sales Director who, on the quiet at least, holds the real power in the company; although in public both men are careful to make sure that it appears to be the other way round.

The Sales Director doesn't really like the Marketing Manager but sees it as part of his job to go for a drink with her twice a month. He is careful not to let her know what he really thinks of her, how dismissive he actually is of her input at management team meetings or that it was he who was the prime mover behind the decision not to let her take charge of the customer services team when the last manager resigned. When going for a drink with her he throws her one or two tidbits of information every now and then to maintain the illusion that he keeps her in the loop, but actually he doesn't tell her anything of any importance.

TURN FOR THE WORSE

By the start of the fifth week of her employment the Customer Services Manager is finding her job stimulating, demanding and stressful. She has too much to do, too little support and wants to set and meet high standards for herself, her team and their work. She is, however, enjoying the social side of life in the office and has developed many warm acquaintanceships during her short time with the company. She regularly spends her coffee breaks with colleagues from the web team, the logistics team and the accounts team. She is popular and sociable, and seems to fit in really well with her new colleagues and workplace contacts.

The Marketing Manager starts to attend some of the coffee breaks. She has never done this before and the Customer Services Manager is initially pleased, hoping that it will provide her with an opportunity to get to know her boss a bit better. However, events take a turn for the worse when the Marketing Manager starts to use these coffee breaks as an opportunity to criticize the Customer Services Manager in front of her colleagues.

Her first critical comments are veiled in dark, slightly cynical humor, but then they move into different territory as she makes belittling and occasionally nasty comments as well. The other people present seem embarrassed and shift uncomfortably in their seats. Having made a comment the Marketing Manager typically waits for a few seconds and then says that she is busy and needs to return to work.

The Customer Services Manager recognizes that her boss is irritated with her but doesn't go and speak to her about it. She has a huge amount of work to get through. She is also wary of giving her boss any opportunity to be unpleasant to her and doesn't think that her boss is likely to listen to her anyway. She determines to continue to do a good job and simply let her boss's irascible comments wash over her head.

Questions For You To Answer: Set Three

Answer the following two questions which examine the issues surrounding the cutting comments which the Marketing Manager makes about the Customer Services Manager during coffee breaks:

- The Customer Services Manager decides not to confront her manager over the belittling comments she makes at coffee breaks. What risks does she run by taking this approach?

- Had the Customer Services Manager decided to speak with her manager about her conduct during coffee breaks how would you advise her to approach the meeting?

IMPROMPTU APPRAISAL

After three months of increasing pressure and increasing workloads, the Customer Services Manager begins to think about asking for a transfer to another role. She does not like working for her boss whose coldness and occasional rudeness, coupled with her unsupportive style, make her a difficult senior colleague to have. There is an opening in the web team and the Customer Services Manager thinks that the more regular work patterns of the web team, plus the more open and sunny style of their manager, would suit her better. However, she worries that should she apply for but not get the role, she would have to continue to work for the Marketing Manager who would know about her failed application and be even more difficult to work with.

On a Wednesday morning she arrives at work and is surprised to find a handwritten note on her desk. The Marketing Manager has left a note which says that she has arranged an impromptu appraisal for the Customer Services Manager and that it will be held that morning at 10 a.m. in her office. The Customer Services Manager is taken aback, not only because she isn't expecting an appraisal for another three months, but also because she doesn't think that a glass-fronted office in an open plan floor is a suitable room in which to hold an appraisal.

The appraisal doesn't go well. The Marketing Manager has a list of 'performance issues' that she wants to raise with the Customer Services Manager. They include concerns about the standard of her work, how often she is away from her team, how late she is at responding to the Marketing Manager's queries and requests for input and how far behind she is getting with the Customer Audit. The Customer Services Manager agrees that she has a lot to do but disagrees that the standard of her work is below expectation. The more that she points out the injustice of the criticisms being made by her boss, the more the Marketing Manager counters with another complaint and another criticism.

The appraisal meeting ends with the two women holding widely differing views on the 'performance issues' that the Marketing Manager raises. As she is leaving her office the Marketing Manager tells the Customer Services Manager that the company is acquiring a smaller drinks-manufacturing unit and that she and her team will have to take over their portfolio of work as well as continue with their existing work. She then turns back to her computer and picks up the telephone. The Customer Services Manager leaves her office feeling dismayed at the content of the impromptu appraisal and worried about how she and her team will be able to cope with yet more work on top of their existing workloads.

Questions For You To Answer: Set Four

Put yourself in the Customer Services Manager's shoes and answer the following two questions:

■ What is your reading of the impromptu appraisal meeting that the Marketing Manager arranges?

■ In what ways does this meeting alter the relationship between the Customer Services Manager and the Marketing Manager?

BUSINESS TRIP

Shortly after setting up the impromptu appraisal the Marketing Manager sets off on a one-week business trip leaving her Customer Services Manager to a pile of additional work. The Customer Services Manager uses her boss's absence to get her head down and plow through the work. She gets a lot done and also finds time to build her relationship with the Sales Director, who she has started to like and trust. Toward the end of the week she conceives of the idea of conveying to him her belief that her manager has recently manufactured a bogus series of criticisms about her and relayed them to her in an unplanned and unnecessary appraisal meeting.

She meets with him on a Friday afternoon at the end of a particularly trying day. During the meeting she agrees to provide him with data on the time it takes the customer services team to resolve complaints and, after going back to her desk to assemble the information, she returns to his office. As she is about to leave his office she turns back to him and takes the opportunity to tell the Sales Director about the bogus appraisal. She describes her manager's behavior during the impromptu appraisal, includes a description of her critical comments at coffee breaks and mentions her reluctance to give the Customer Services Manager any time.

The Sales Director hears her out and then tells her that he has to make a call but will get back to her the following week. The Customer Services Manager feels relieved that she has, at last, told someone in authority about some of the things that her manager has been doing and goes home in a happier frame of mind than she had done for weeks.

THE START OF THE WEEK

The Customer Services Manager arrives in the office at 9.10 a.m. on Monday morning and sees that the Sales Director is speaking with the Marketing Manager in her glass-panelled office. She hopes that they are talking about the impromptu appraisal and her more general feedback to the Sales Director about her boss's behavior. The meeting ends just before 10 a.m. and the Marketing Manager spends the rest of the morning in her glass-fronted office, head down at her desk. Nothing is said to the Customer Services Manager by either of the two senior managers, and the week ends without the Sales Director having got back to her as promised.

The following month the Customer Services Manager takes annual leave and goes away with her family for a short break. She returns home on Saturday to find a message from her boss on her home telephone informing her that she is expected in a meeting which is set to begin at 9 a.m. on Monday morning in the Conference Room. The Customer Services Manager is surprised as the Conference Room is reserved for executive meetings only.

UNEXPECTED ATTACK

The Customer Services Manager arrives a few minutes after 9 a.m. having dropped her children off early at school. She hurries to the Conference Room and, on entering it, is surprised to see the Marketing Manager seated alongside a human resources manager whom she had met during the selection process. Her manager speaks to her in a cold tone and tells her to sit down. She then begins the meeting by telling her team leader that she is the subject of a formal review meeting occasioned by her below par performance.

The Customer Services Manager simply doesn't know what to say to her boss and is stunned at this turn of events. The Marketing Manager outlines a series of complaints about the standard of the Customer Services Manager's work, providing dates and times of supposed misdemeanors which range from 'being late' to 'providing inaccurate feedback about her conduct to the Sales Director'. She refers to the previous appraisal she conducted and claims that the 'performance issues' that she had outlined during that meeting were still unaddressed. The Customer Services Manager tries to defend herself against these allegations but, without having had time to prepare, is on the back foot from the start.

The meeting lasts two hours and, at its conclusion, the human resources manager hands her a two-page letter. The formally worded letter informs her that she is 'on notice' and that her performance will be reviewed again in three months' time.

Questions For You To Answer: Set Five

Put yourself in the Customer Services Manager's shoes and answer the following four questions:

- What is your reading of the background to the formal review meeting that the Marketing Manager instigates?

- In what specific ways does the Customer Services Manager mishandle her relationship with the Sales Director in the lead up to the formal review meeting?

- What could the Customer Services Manager have done differently and better to enable her to handle the formal review meeting more effectively?

■ What conclusions can you draw from this case study?

```



```

Review Section: Answers to the Questions

The final section of the case study provides a summary of the key issues from the Customer Services Manager's point of view. Each of the bullet points below relates, in order, to each of the questions above. You might like to read each answer and compare it with the notes that you jotted down.

Set One

■ Had she decided to respond to it at the time, how would you advise the Customer Services Manager to reply to the Marketing Manager's comment that the two of them 'will get along fine'?

This is an ambiguous comment and one which is said to the Customer Services Manager early in their working relationship by her new boss. The Marketing Manager is a somewhat aloof and cool character so a suggestion that she and a new colleague will 'get along fine' can't be taken at face value or simply left unanswered. While its meaning isn't explicit, the Customer Services Manager can make a good guess that it isn't the friendly overture that these words would have been, had they been said by someone with a more open and sunny disposition.

So what does it mean? It is probable that the Marketing Manager is putting a marker down; one that conveys to the Customer Services Manager that she *expects* to get along fine with her new colleague as long as her new colleague handles the relationship along lines that are sufficiently comfortable for the Market Manager. It's not quite 'I am the boss' but more a warning that says 'I advise you to respect me and my position here'.

How should the Customer Services Manager respond? She has two choices: she can make a reply or ask a question. Saying nothing is not wise as it will encourage the Marketing Manager to continue with her embryonic tactic of making veiled comments, comments which receive no comeback or countering remark to dissuade her from making them in future.

If the Customer Services Manager wants to make a reply she could say in a friendly and open tone 'I also hope we establish a positive working relationship' or 'Lets hope so, I'm looking forward to finding my feet around here'. But perhaps the more useful thing she could say would be to ask her manager to elaborate. She could say 'I hope we do get along fine. What would that involve from your point of view?' This is an open question inviting her manager to outline what she is looking for from the Customer Services Manager as they work together. The response should provide the Customer Services Manager with important information about where her new manager draws the line and what expectations she has of her new team leader. Armed with this information the Customer Services Manager can then make some decisions about how to handle her relationship with her new boss.

■ Had she decided to respond at the time, how would you advise the Customer Services Manager to reply to her boss's subsequent comment that 'there is a clear meeting of minds' between the two of them?

This is another comment that needs a reply as there clearly isn't a 'meeting of minds' between them. Firstly, they haven't worked more than three days together and during that time they haven't spent enough time together to establish the kind of bond that could be characterized as a 'meeting of minds'. Secondly, they have widely differing values. The Marketing Manager is reserved and status conscious. The Customer Services Manager is interpersonally able and warm.

So what could this comment mean? It is probable that the Marketing Manager is putting down a second marker straight after the first one. First she tells the Customer Services Manager to respect her and her position, and then tells her that she sees her new team leader as someone in her own mold. This is an extraordinary comment to make but it is also very revealing. The Marketing Manager *wants* to get on well with the Customer Services Manager but will only be able to do so if the Customer Services Manager handles the relationship in ways which suit the Marketing Manager. As a character she is only able to extend trust to someone over whom she has power. Clearly she has greater organizational status than the Customer Services Manager, but what she really wants is the Customer Services Manager's personal respect. This is something she cannot command but needs to have extended to her by the Customer Services Manager. The implication is that if the Customer Services Manager defers sufficiently to the Marketing Manager's will they will get along fine; but if she doesn't they won't.

How should the Customer Services Manager respond? She needs to find something to say to enable her to remain as an active participant in the conversation and avoid characterizing herself as the passive recipient of the Marketing Manager's veiled remarks. She could say in an open and friendly tone 'I haven't come to that conclusion yet, but that doesn't mean that we won't see eye to eye' or 'I'm glad you think so' to show that while her boss might have come to that conclusion she hasn't. Equally, she could simply put the ball back into her court by asking her, kindly and politely, what she has observed that leads her to the conclusion that there is a meeting of minds between them.

■ What interpretation do you form about the Marketing Manager's motivation for saying these two things?

These are important moments in the evolving relationship between the Marketing Manager and the Customer Services Manager. The Marketing Manager waits until day three of the new Customer Services Manager's employment before making these two revealing comments to her new employee, three days in which she has observed her new colleague interacting with colleagues around the office.

The Marketing Manager sees herself as the most influential woman in the firm, a role she highly prizes and takes pride in. However, the new Customer Services Manager is also female and is more interpersonally skilled and warm than the Marketing Manager. She is therefore a potential rival for the role of most influential person in the company. But the Customer Services Manager's more informal influence will come from the fact that people like her and not from the fact that they are frightened of her as with the Marketing Manager. The Marketing Manager notes all this and is discomforted to say the least.

She notes how easily the Customer Services Manager gets on with people she hasn't met before, and how quickly she establishes rapport with her new colleagues. These are skills and abilities she lacks and which she envies in those who have developed them. The Marketing Manager feels envious of her new team leader's personal qualities and determines that, should the Customer Services Manager get too above herself, she will clip her wings. She uses the meeting on day three to lay down a clear marker: get too big for your boots and I will cut you down to size.

Set Two

■ The Customer Services Manager responds to her manager's e-mail with an e-mail of her own. But she doesn't go and talk the issue through with the Marketing Manager. What would have been the potential benefits to her of talking the issue through face-to-face?

It would have helped her cause had the Customer Services Manager chosen to talk with her boss about the issues raised in her e-mail. By responding in an e-mail she avoids the opportunity to speak with her boss and establish a dialogue with her. The Customer Services Manager could have gone to the Marketing Manager's office and, looking her boss fairly and squarely in the eye, used a firm and not unfriendly tone to point out that her contract allows her to arrive before 9.30 a.m.; that traffic has delayed her recently; and that she too wants to arrive earlier than she has done. She could then ask 'Is there anything specific that is on your mind?'

This approach would have laid down a clear marker of her own and put the ball respectfully back into her boss's court. It would have acknowledged the complaint made by the Marketing Manager but also made the point that she doesn't really have valid grounds to complain. It would have recognized that there may well be something specific that is worrying her, something that makes the complaint reasonable. The Marketing Manager would have been forced to confront the fact that, if there isn't, she really hasn't got a valid reason to complain.

It also demonstrates to the Marketing Manager that her team leader is not thrown or intimidated by the tactic of a complaint made on e-mail and is quite comfortable talking with her about the issues.

- Even though the Marketing Manager partially retracts her initial e-mail by acknowledging that the Customer Services Manager does stay late, she is still clearly irritated at something. What could account for her need to pick her team leader up on her timekeeping which, on the face of it, isn't poor?

The Marketing Manager sends her e-mail to the Customer Services Manager out of her growing jealousy and envy at her team leader's popularity around the office. In her mind she begins to characterize her as someone who is a slacker and who, if not watched, will arrive late for work. The Marketing Manager is also concerned about the Sales Director's growing approval for the new Customer Services Manager's work and attitude around the office. The Marketing Manager doesn't like this fact either and determines to have a go at her new team leader in retaliation. There isn't anything in her work that she can attack her over, so she manufactures a bogus complaint instead and sends her an e-mail about her timekeeping.

Set Three

- The Customer Services Manager decides not to confront her manager over the belittling comments she makes at coffee breaks. What risks does she run by taking this approach?

The Customer Services Manager makes a mistake by not rebutting these comments. She hopes that the obvious discomfort of the other employees present at the coffee breaks will be sufficient to dissuade the Marketing Manager from making any further snide comments about her in public. But she misunderstands the nature of the Marketing Manager who isn't at all concerned about what her junior colleagues might think of her. Rather than feel that she has misbehaved in public, she is emboldened to continue to find ways of humiliating the Customer Services Manager both publicly and in private. She is motivated by her growing envy of her team leader and by the fact that the Customer Services Manager doesn't create any consequences for her to deal with as a result of making undermining comments about her in public.

■ Had the Customer Services Manager decided to speak with her manager about her conduct during coffee breaks how would you advise her to approach the meeting?

This is the first open example of behavior which, should it become part of a campaign, could be characterized as bullying behavior. The Customer Services Manager could have gone to her boss's office later that day and told her that while she was quite willing to be ticked off for things she could do differently, it would be better if she drew the line at having belittling comments made about her in the office. She needs to keep her voice steady, her demeanor calm and her tone firm and even throughout.

Set Four

■ What is your reading of the impromptu appraisal meeting that the Marketing Manager arranges?

This is a bogus appraisal in which the Marketing Manager raises a series of flimsy 'performance issues' to undermine and humiliate the Customer Services Manager. Her criticisms are unclear and a matter of subjective opinion, and there is no clear evidence to back up any of them. The two women argue about the rights and wrongs of each issue. No resolution can be found to any of the complaints made against the Customer Services Manager because there aren't any real grounds to support any of them. The more she argues the more the Marketing Manager generates another bogus angle on the complaint or introduces another distorted perception as 'evidence' of her case against the Customer Services Manager. They go round and round in exhausting circles.

The 'impromptu appraisal' is a power play designed to impress upon the Customer Services Manager that the Marketing Manager is the one who has the official, organizational power in the office, even if her team leader has the unofficial, popular vote. The 'impromptu appraisal' is motivated by the Marketing Manager's envy of her junior colleague and is an example of her passive-aggressive nature. It is purely a vehicle for her animosity toward her junior colleague, a vehicle which gives her an opportunity to attack her colleague over something in which she takes pride: her performance.

- In what ways does this meeting alter the relationship between the Customer Services Manager and the Marketing Manager?

This meeting changes their relationship from one in which the Marketing Manager attacks the personal qualities of the Customer Services Manager in public into one in which she attacks her *work*. This is an escalation of her vendetta against her colleague and should be a clear warning to the Customer Services Manager that she is the subject of a sustained, personalized assault by her manager.

Set Five

- What is your reading of the background to the formal review meeting that the Marketing Manager instigates?

Unwittingly, the Customer Services Manager makes things worse for herself by confiding in the Sales Director. She lets the cordial nature of her relationship with the Sales Director cloud her judgment. She assumes that he will be highly motivated to prevent the Marketing Manager from continuing to abuse her position and manufacture bogus complaints against the Customer Services Manager. Unfortunately for the Customer Services Manager this isn't the case at all. The Sales Director tells her that he will get back to her but doesn't. Instead, first thing on Monday morning, he goes to talk to the Marketing Manager about the allegations made against her. He tells the Marketing Manager what has been said about her by the Customer Services Manager and thereby, intentionally or not, increases her power.

The Marketing Manager is actually quite comfortable with this turn of events. When speaking face-to-face with the Sales Director the Marketing Manager says that she will sort it all out. Behind his back she renews her campaign against the Customer Services Manager with even more vigor. She now knows that her undermining tactics have succeeded in intimidating the Customer Services Manager so much that she has sought support from one of the most senior people in the company – and at a time when she, the Marketing Manager, was on a business trip. This is the green light for her to renew her attack – after a suitable period of time – and she plans and implements a formal review meeting to humiliate the Customer Services Manager.

■ In what specific ways does the Customer Services Manager mishandle her relationship with the Sales Director in the lead up to the formal review meeting?

The Customer Services Manager believes, wrongly, that the Sales Director will make it his job as a senior figure in the company to root out any behavior which is underhand or devious. These two characteristics are not in her nature, and she wrongly assumes that the Sales Director, who is cordial and warm when working with her, will be motivated to confront these destructive behaviors on her behalf. She doesn't realize that he is just as political as the Marketing Manager, albeit his political activity is centered around his relationship with his boss the CEO. She also doesn't realize that he doesn't like the Marketing Manager who is a woman with whom he spends time reluctantly. She doesn't know that the kinds of passive-aggressive behaviors she complains of are exactly the kinds of passive-aggressive behaviors he employs with the CEO.

In the end she shoots herself in the foot by trying to enlist his help. The only thing the Sales Director judges the Marketing Manager on is whether or not she meets her targets. He doesn't care how she reaches them. He only cares that she does. He goes to see the Marketing Manager to talk through the allegations made against her and give her an opportunity to put in her side of the story. It never occurs to him that this will place the Customer Services Manager in an invidious position. The Marketing Manager handles her interview with him well enough. He turns a blind eye to her methods, enabling her to escalate her campaign against the Customer Services Manager should she want to.

■ What could the Customer Services Manager have done differently and better to enable her to handle the formal review meeting more effectively?

This meeting is all about power and who has it. In order to handle it well the Customer Services Manager needs to employ self-protective tactics and use assertive behavior. She needs, at some point in the meeting, to take steps specifically designed to regain some measure of control for herself in the meeting.

The Marketing Manager has set the meeting up so that, initially, she retains maximum power for herself. Firstly, it is a meeting to which she invites her team leader on her return from holiday. She doesn't tell her Customer Services Manager what the meeting is about or why she is being invited to it. She certainly doesn't tell her that her performance is the sole topic of discussion for the meeting. Secondly, her invitation is issued to the Customer Services Manager's answering machine at home, for her to pick up on her return from holiday. This is a deliberate ploy by the Marketing Manager designed to catch her junior colleague off guard while she is still in holiday mode, relaxed and off duty. Thirdly, the meeting is being held in the Conference Room, a senior meeting room usually reserved for executive level meetings. This, in and of itself, will put the Customer Services Manager at a disadvantage as it smacks of prestige and status. Fourthly, the Marketing Manager makes sure that an HR manager is present at the meeting, again unknown to the Customer Services Manager, to reinforce the fact that the meeting is formal and disciplinary in nature. Fifthly, the agenda for the meeting is a surprise appraisal which the Customer Services Manager is not expecting and for which she has no time to prepare.

Given all this, how should the Customer Services Manager handle the meeting? She needs to realize that it is primarily about power and handle it accordingly. The specific 'performance issues' under discussion are a rouse designed to give the Marketing Manager an opportunity to criticize her. In order to protect herself she needs to retain control as much as possible. She could interrupt the Marketing Manager's momentum by standing up and getting a drink of water for herself from the drinks cabinet. She could then offer a drink to her two colleagues while she is there. Alternatively, she could stand up and go to move the blind up or down, or open or close the curtains in the room. She could simply get up and walk around, claiming to need to stretch her legs. All of these tactics will break the Marketing Manager's flow and give her an opportunity to take back control of the meeting. She then needs to use the opportunity she has created well.

She could go onto the front foot by saying, clearly and calmly, that she wasn't expecting an appraisal and hadn't been informed that she would be having one. She needs to say that she'd like written details of each of the 'performance issues' under discussion and time to prepare a reply to each of them. She needs to say that she is surprised at what is happening and that she would like to know why someone from human resources is being included in the meeting. If she doesn't get answers that she can work with she needs to consider leaving the meeting and returning to her desk. No doubt she will hear more about it but this approach will protect her from the greater injustice of having to discuss her 'performance issues' for two hours in front of a colleague from HR and without having had any time to gather the facts she needs to challenge the lies being told about her.

- What conclusions can you draw from this case study?

Firstly, at no point in the action described above does the Customer Services Manager see her manager's behavior for what it is: a growing campaign of workplace bullying. She fails to recognize it for what it is and sees her manager's passive-aggression toward her as 'the way she does things'. It is, of course, the way she does things but it is much more than that. The Customer Services Manager doesn't look beyond the surface behavior of her manager to identify what motivates her. She doesn't see the dynamics between them or look beyond the obvious, and she thereby leaves herself vulnerable to a clever and sustained campaign of workplace bullying.

Secondly, her manager's bullying is particularly difficult to handle because it starts so insidiously and escalates so suddenly. The Customer Services Manager doesn't have many warnings before she finds herself in an invidious position: working for a woman who is envious of her, abusive toward her and able to continue her campaign against her even though the Sales Director, her boss, has been told about it.

Thirdly, the Customer Services Manager is further disadvantaged in that she doesn't realize that the Sales Director routinely undermines the CEO; or that he keeps his boss in a job by doing his work for him. She also doesn't know that the reason the last Customer Services Manager left the company was that she so disliked the style of the Marketing Manager, a style that was both status conscious and punitive.

Fourthly, the Customer Services Manager needs to handle her boss differently from day one if she is to stand any chance of preventing her manager from introducing a bullying dynamic into their relationship. The Marketing Manager's bullying behavior is consistent: she makes unjustified, abusive complaints about the Customer Services Manager whether in an e-mail, over coffee, in a bogus appraisal or to HR colleagues. To stand any chance of countering this behavior the Customer Services Manager needs to respond to each and every instance or else her boss will gain encouragement and continue to use the behavior.

Fifthly, the longer the Customer Services Manager stays in her role and doesn't effectively challenge her manager, the more power her manager will erode from her and the easier it will be for her to act unopposed. At no point in the action does the naturally kind and sociable Customer Services Manager confront her manager over her behavior. It is not an easy thing to confront one's manager but, in some instances, like the one above, it is imperative. The alternative is to continue to work for a manager who constantly issues bogus complaints and whose ruthlessness grows as she realizes that she can do so without any consequences being laid upon her.

Lastly, by asking for help from a senior manager whom she doesn't know well and of whose motives she cannot be sure, the Customer Services Manager, sadly, hands the initiative to the Marketing Manager. Her actions incense her boss who takes them as a personal betrayal. Most managers would know that it is unreasonable to expect a team member to demonstrate personal loyalty toward them when they consistently injure that team member. But the Marketing Manager isn't reasonable. She does expect personal loyalty from the Customer Services manager and is furious when she complains about her behind her back. She is clever enough to wait awhile before taking her revenge but when she does it is simply devastating. The Customer Services Manager is left with two options: continue to work for a woman motivated to set up a lengthy series of subsequent formal review meetings at which she will pick holes in her team leader's performance – or resign to save herself from further humiliation. Neither option is palatable although one of them will at least prevent her from incurring further personal damage.

SUMMARY AND NEXT CHAPTER

This chapter has taken the form of a case study which has highlighted the dangers of failing to confront a potentially bullying boss early on in a working relationship. It has also highlighted the issues faced when a good natured employee fails to see bullying behavior for what it is, and misguidedly trusts a senior manager who isn't prepared to act on her behalf.

The case study has discussed various strategies that you could use should you find yourself on the receiving end of passive-aggressive tactics similar to those employed by the Marketing Manager.

The next chapter explores the emotional, psychological and physical consequences that you might expect should you become subject to a campaign of bullying behavior at work.

CHAPTER 9

The Human Consequences of Bullying at Work
Common Emotional, Psychological and Physical Reactions to Workplace Bullying

We have examined many, many aspects of bullying behavior at work. But one thing we have not considered is the human cost to those of you who have been, or are being bullied. Let's now do just that. This chapter will examine some of the emotional, psychological and physical consequences you might experience should you be subject to workplace bullying. The aim of the chapter is to help those of you who think that you might be subject to workplace bullying to assess the impact of your experiences and determine what you could do to help yourself.

This chapter will:

- Identify a range of emotional and psychological consequences you might experience as a result of being subject to workplace bullying.
- Highlight a range of physical reactions you might expect as a consequence of being subject to workplace bullying.
- Outline a series of practical steps you can take to support yourself through your experience of being bullied at work.
- Suggest that some of you might consider talking though your experiences with a professional skilled at helping people subject to workplace bullying.

DIFFERENT PEOPLE, DIFFERENT REACTIONS

You think you are being bullied at work. You are clear that what is happening to you is both deeply personal and punishing. You want to understand just how the bullying is likely to impact you emotionally, psychologically and physically as you continue to be subject to it.

Different people react differently to workplace bullying and there is no typical reaction. Some of you will feel badly shaken – even traumatized – straight away. Others will take longer to feel bad about what is happening to you and some of you won't register the full consequences of what you are experiencing for several weeks or months. It all depends on:

- Your temperament.
- Your individual experiences of bullying behavior.
- The extent to which you are able to remain objective in the face of the bullying, rather than turning it in on yourself.
- The extent to which you are able to find effective sources of support during your experience of bullying, either professionally or from friends and family.

Those of you who face a constant drip-feed of critical comments and undermining, snide remarks may react differently to those of you who experience periodic, powerful aggression. Those of you who are bullied by someone with whom you had a positive working relationship prior to the bullying commencing might react differently to those of you who are bullied by someone you've not worked with before.

Consider the following examples:

- A graphic designer is subject to workplace bullying from a former close coworker with whom he previously had a positive working relationship. Being a robust character he doesn't initially register any ill-effects, although he is shocked and upset that his erstwhile friendly colleague could be so unpleasant to him. He still feels able and willing to go to work, and while he sleeps longer during the weekend, he doesn't notice himself reacting any differently to normal. That is until three weeks into the experience of workplace bullying when he wakes up with a blinding headache and vomits as soon as he gets up. He calls in sick that day and takes the next day off as well. When he returns to work two days later he feels tired all day and lacks his usual energy, a set of symptoms which continues throughout his experience of being bullied, as does a growing sense that his former coworker has betrayed their workplace friendship.
- An administrative assistant in a library is subject to workplace bullying by her manager. From day one she feels weepy and stressed. She leaves work and cries on the bus on the way home, doesn't eat anything that evening and returns to work the next day feeling apprehensive and fearful. Feeling unable to defend herself against her bullying boss she feels vulnerable to further bullying. She experiences high levels of anxiety every time she sees him or has to speak

to him. After three days she visits her doctor and is signed off work
with stress.

- A customer services consultant in a retail bank call center is subject
to workplace bullying by his team leader. For the first three days of
being bullied he doesn't notice any untoward physical or emotional
reactions but, on the fourth day, he wakes up and doesn't want to go
to work. He feels angry and irritable instead of his usual optimistic
self, and he notices that the skin on his back is itchy and red. Over
the next two weeks the eczema spreads to his shoulders and arms
and he finds it difficult to concentrate at work.

Common Emotional and Psychological
Reactions to Workplace Bullying

So what might be the emotional and psychological reactions you could
experience should you be subject to workplace bullying? You might
want to review the following list of common emotional and psychological reactions to being bullied at work and identify how many of
them you recognize in yourself. You can jot these down in the space
below the list. The list is not exhaustive and you might also note down
any additional emotional or psychological reactions that you recognize in yourself in the same space.

The list headings are adapted from 'Factsheet on Workplace Bullying'
which is available from the Andrea Adams Trust website:

- *Feeling anxiety:* You might experience anxiety as a result of being
subject to workplace bullying. Your anxiety could be acute or mild
or somewhere in between. It could cause you to feel anything from
apprehension or uneasiness about going to work or meeting the person
bullying you, to full-on dread and distress at either of these prospects.
- *Feeling isolated and alone:* You may also feel unusually separate
from normal life. Even though you are doing normal things – going
to work, living as a part of society, socializing – it's as if your experiences set you apart from other people and you feel alone even when
you are in company. This might be doubly true if you cannot bring
yourself to confide in anyone about what is happening to you at
work or if the people you turn to don't react in ways you find supportive or helpful.
- *Losing confidence:* Being the subject of a sustained campaign of individual assaults which are difficult to predict and against which you
cannot easily defend yourself, can sap your confidence. You may feel
less assured than you used to and have less belief in yourself than

you had before the bullying began. You may feel less able to handle the daily stresses and strains of life. You may be less prepared to rely on your judgement or trust your intuitions in comparison to before the bullying started. All this can result in you losing confidence and starting to doubt yourself.

■ *Losing self-esteem:* You may also find that you think less of yourself than you did before you became subject to workplace bullying. You may simply see yourself as less able or less competent than you used to, or you might start to think that you deserve what is happening to you at work. Some of you might start to believe that your life doesn't really matter that much and that what is happening isn't worth making a fuss about.

■ *Feeling angry:* You may feel uncharacteristically angry about what is happening to you or you may experience sudden feelings of rage even if you aren't thinking about the person who is bullying you. You might find that your temper fuse is shorter than usual or that you become irritable and snappy much more easily than you would have done prior to being bullied.

■ *Experiencing mood swings:* You might find that your mood swings uncharacteristically from even-tempered to morose or from angry to bitter and that the force of the swings takes you by surprise. You may never have experienced mood swings like this before and may find them hard to understand. Some of your moods may be so powerful that they threaten to overwhelm you.

■ *Lacking energy or motivation:* You might simply not see much point in doing anything or going anywhere, either because you haven't got the energy or you don't see the point. You might feel tired and listless all the time and simply not want to do much.

■ *Feeling depressed:* You may be slipping into an experience of depression. You might feel despondent about yourself or your future or you may feel pessimistic and sad most of or all of the time. You may feel fatigued and lethargic, lose your appetite and have trouble getting to sleep or staying asleep. You may wake up early in the morning. During the day you may find it difficult to concentrate or think for any period of time, and experience higher levels of anxiety than you normally would.

Common Physical Reactions to Workplace Bullying

In addition to the emotional and psychological consequences outlined above you may also experience a range of physical symptoms as well. Many of these symptoms are as a result of experiencing higher than normal levels of anxiety. The acid test is whether or not you regularly experienced these symptoms prior to becoming subject to workplace bullying. Take a look at the following list of common physical reactions to workplace bullying and identify how many of them you recognize in yourself. You can jot these down in the space below the list. Once again, the list is not exhaustive so you might also note down any additional physical reactions that you recognize in yourself that are not included on the list.

The following list headings are adapted from 'Factsheet on Workplace Bullying' which is available from the Andrea Adams Trust website:

- *Feeling nauseous*: You might feel sick all the time or some of the time, either in the pit of your stomach or in your throat. You may actually be sick as well even though you don't have a stomach bug or any other illness that might explain your vomiting.
- *Developing headaches or migraines*: You might find that you wake up with a headache or migraine or develop one on going to work. You might find that your headache or migraine coincides with times when you are due to meet the bully or is there when you get home every evening.
- *Developing palpitations*: You might feel that your heart starts to beat much quicker than usual every now and then and that this causes you to feel panicky and afraid. You might find it difficult to get your breath when your heart races.
- *Developing skin conditions*: Your skin might become sore and itchy and you might develop a stress-related skin condition such as eczema or psoriasis. Your skin might also break out in blotches.
- *Developing backache*: Your back might start to ache, and no matter how often you shift in your seat or alter your stance, it continues to do so.
- *Sweating or shaking*: You might start to experience excessive sweating or shaking or both, and feel unable to stop either symptom from reoccurring. You might sweat from your palms, or scalp or underarms, and your hands or torso might tremor.
- *Losing your appetite*: You might simply not want to eat anything and find that you lose your appetite. Not eating means that you don't take in the nutrients you need through your food, and this

can further weaken you and reduce your energy and ability to concentrate.

■ *Reduced immune system efficiency*: You might find yourself more and more prone to colds, infections and viruses as your immune system struggles to cope with the assault upon your well-being and can't resist bugs and illnesses as effectively as it usually would.

SEEKING PROFESSIONAL HELP

Many people who are subject to workplace bullying feel ashamed that they are being bullied and some don't confide in anyone. Those of you who are trying to struggle on alone might not be doing the best you could for yourselves. Should you recognize some or all of the symptoms listed above – and maybe others besides – you might want to consider getting professional help from a counselor, coach, psychologist, therapist or psychiatrist skilled at helping people with the issues caused by workplace bullying.

Getting help sooner rather than later can help you:

■ Take stock of what is happening to you.
■ Understand how your experience is affecting you emotionally, psychologically and physically.
■ Identify coping strategies that could assist you in dealing with the bullying behavior and its consequences for you.
■ Help you feel less isolated and more supported.
■ Reduce the level of suffering you experience as a result of being bullied at work.

The earlier you seek help the more likely it will be that you can successfully put in place coping strategies that will help you obviate some of the more damaging effects of bullying that you might otherwise experience should you become beleaguered later on. Don't let yourself get isolated. There is no shame in being bullied. The true shame lies with the bully, not with you.

HELPING YOURSELF THROUGH IT

Whether or not you decide to seek professional help there are a number of simple, effective steps you can take to support yourself through an experience of workplace bullying. These include:

- *Find someone to talk to*: Stay connected to life and don't let yourself become isolated. Talk to your friends and family about what is going on at work and, if they don't respond the way you need, consider approaching a skilled professional instead. Don't bottle up how you are feeling – it will not help you in the long run.
- *Record what is happening to you*: You might want to keep a written, voice-taped or computer record of what is happening to you at work and what it means to you. The section entitled 'Practical Things You Can Do To Help' in Chapter 7 contains an exercise that you might want to carry out daily which will enable you to process the incidents from that day and determine how they have affected you.
- *Eat a balanced diet*: This is easier said than done if you have lost your appetite, but it is vital that you ingest the full range of nutrients your body needs to function effectively. Make sure you eat proteins, carbohydrates and roughage, preferably with lots of fruits, green vegetables and salad stuff, as well as have plenty of water to drink. If you have genuinely lost your appetite and really can't face anything get some good quality vitamin and mineral supplements to take while you're not eating normally.
- *Exercise*: Exercising is a great way of processing emotion without having to think it through consciously. Jog, walk briskly, play squash, go to the gym, spend time in the countryside or park or walk your dog.
- *Plan treats for yourself*: The best affirmation you can give yourself during this difficult time is self-affirmation. So plan to spend time doing what you enjoy, both inside and outside your home. Keep this commitment to yourself and make it a priority.
- *Contact your doctor*: Keep your doctor appraised of what you are going through even if you don't think you need medication.

SUMMARY AND NEXT CHAPTER

This chapter has highlighted some of the emotional, psychological and physical reactions you can expect should you be subject to workplace bullying. It has also:

- Outlined some practical steps that might bolster you as you go through an experience of workplace bullying.

- Suggested that some of you may need to consult a professional skilled at working with people who have been bullied in their workplace.

The following chapter concludes our discussion of how to handle, manage and respond to incidents of workplace bullying. Its aim is to focus your mind on the key messages in the book and on the reality of life after an experience of workplace bullying.

CHAPTER 10

Aftermath
Final Thoughts on Workplace Bullying

LIFE AFTER BEING BULLIED AT WORK

Workplace bullying affects thousands and thousands of you each year. It is on the increase and, sadly, more and more people witness it, are subject to it and are affected by it in workplaces everywhere. However, without in anyway wishing to reduce an experience of workplace bullying, it is possible to recover from the punishing effects of bullying behavior and find enjoyment and satisfaction at work.

Consider the following examples:

- A primary school teacher is subject to workplace bullying by one of the senior teachers in her school. She watches two of her colleagues resign as a result of widespread bullying in the school and, after failing to find help from the governors in charge of the school, she also decides to resign. This is a difficult decision for her to make as she has worked all her life as a teacher and worries that she is abandoning her colleagues to the bullying culture at school. She seeks the advice of a counsellor to help her process her experiences and find relief from the consequences of workplace bullying. She then retrains as therapist. Today she works with people who have been bullied at work and helps them handle their experiences and find release from them.
- A PA to a manager in a large risk management consultancy is subject to constant workplace bullying by her boss. In fact her boss routinely bullies everyone in her team. The PA keeps her head down and gets on with her work, determined not to let her boss get to her. She decides that the best way to handle the bullying behavior she is subject to is to let it wash over her head. She recognizes that her boss is guilty of systematic bullying and refuses to take it personally. She doesn't argue with her boss, get angry at the way she is being treated, complain to her about her behavior or let the standard of her work slip. Her boss continues to make belittling and cutting

comments when she speaks with her, and continues to use a cold and harsh tone in all her dealings with her. But, somehow, knowing that she isn't able to rock her PA – in fact, knowing that her tactics don't seem to affect her at all – eventually causes the manager to think again. She becomes tired of trying to provoke a reaction in her colleague and reduces the frequency of her bullying behavior toward her. The PA decides that she has the moral victory and asks for a transfer. She is initially refused the right to move jobs but persists with three more applications. Her fourth application is accepted and she is moved to another department where she enjoys her work and her colleagues much more.

- An HR advisor is subject to workplace bullying at the hospital at which she works. She is devastated by the experience and by the collusion of her departmental manager. After 18 months of relentless bullying she seeks help from a psychiatrist and a coach. She takes time off work and assimilates the new perspectives and learning she gains from working with these two advisors. One helps her with her mental well-being and the other helps her to find more productive ways of handling bullying behavior. The HR advisor returns to work and, in her first one-to-one meeting with her assailant, handles herself and him with greater aplomb and assertiveness than she used to do. Her foe is visibly discomforted by her new, more confident approach and she slowly takes charge of the meeting. At a suitable point in the proceedings she sits back in her chair, makes herself as big as possible and tells the colleague sitting opposite her in a calm and measured tone: 'I don't quite trust you'. She watches the colour drain from his face as she regains her power and self-confidence. From that moment onward his bullying behavior toward her simply ceases.

- An assistant editor in a local newspaper is subject to workplace bullying by his editor. He is appalled that he could be on the receiving end of such aggression, and while he realizes that his colleagues are also embarrassed at the behavior of the editor, he is also distressed to realize that none of them come to his aid. He endures the bullying for six months and then decides that enough is enough. He resigns, sells his house and relocates 140 kilometres away to a part of the country in which he has always wanted to live. He rents a small flat and funds himself from the proceeds of his house sale while he retrains as a teacher. He finds a job locally and enjoys the kind of work-life balance that he was unable to have while working in his previous role. In his new role he takes on responsibility for mentoring newly qualified teachers. He makes a point of treating each of the people he is mentoring with respect, giving them his undivided time and attention and investing heavily in the quality of the relationships he builds with them. His experience of workplace bullying is the catalyst for his commitment to people-centered values. He is determined to treat his new colleagues with dignity and consideration: the opposite way to how he was treated by the editor when he was employed at the local newspaper.

PUTTING IT INTO PERSPECTIVE

Being subject to workplace bullying is among the more horrible workplace experiences you might have. It can leave you feeling angry, overwhelmed and vulnerable. It can cause you to become ill and, if you don't find the kind of support you need when you need it, it can result in finding that your life is becoming unmanageable.

But it can also be a catalyst for you to reappraise what you want from life. It can provide you with the impetus to make changes that enhance your life, your work and your well-being. It can enable you to learn and grow, acquiring new and more assertive ways to handle bullying behavior and gain – or regain – your self-confidence and self-belief.

Whatever your experiences of workplace bullying I hope that reading this book has helped you to step back from your workplace and:

- Better understand the complex interpersonal dynamics at the heart of an experience of workplace bullying.
- Consider the situation you find yourself in.
- Assess the options before you.
- Evaluate different strategies and tactics that you could use to protect yourself from bullying behavior at work.
- Select and employ the strategies and tactics that you think will work most effectively for you.

YOUR EXPERIENCES OF WORKPLACE BULLYING

I'd like very much to hear about your experiences of identifying, responding to and managing bullying behavior in the workplace. The following page will provide you with details of how to get in touch with me. Whatever your experiences of workplace bullying, I hope that it has been helpful for you to read this book. I hope that those of you who are the friends and family of someone subject to workplace bullying will be better placed to offer meaningful support to your loved one. I hope that those of you who are responsible for managing a team member who uses bullying behavior will feel better equipped to confront them effectively and consistently until you bring about the resolution you want. Above all, I hope that those of you who work alongside, for or with a workplace bully will have acquired the know-how and interpersonal strategies you need to handle the bullying behavior effectively so that you can continue to feel in charge of what you say, do and feel in the workplace.

Aryanne Oade

To tell me about your experiences of identifying, responding to and managing bullying behavior in your workplace, or to explore options to help you develop further skills in these areas, visit www.oadeassociates.com.

References, Websites and Further Reading

REFERENCES

Chapter One   What is Workplace Bullying?

Corporate Services, University of Ballarat, Australia, has identified a number of behaviors used by workplace bullies. Details of their work can be found at the following link: http://www.ballarat.edu.au/vco/legal/bullying_prevention_and_management.shtml#Definition

Chapter Five   Resisting a Workplace Bully

A. Oade (2009) *Managing Politics at Work: The Essential Toolkit for Identifying and Managing Political Behaviour in the Workplace* (Palgrave Macmillan) ISBN 978-0-230-59541-5.

Chapter Nine   The Human Consequences of Bullying at Work

The Andrea Adams Trust 'Factsheet on Workplace Bullying' available free at www.andreaadamstrust.org.

USEFUL WEBSITES

www.andreaadamstrust.org.
The Andrea Adams Trust is the world's first nonpolitical, nonprofit-making charity operating as the focus for the diverse and complex problems caused by bullying behavior in the workplace.
www.bullyonline.org.
http://www.bullyonline.org/workbully/usa.htm.
http://www.bullyonline.org/workbully/canada.htm.
Bully OnLine is the world's largest resource on workplace bullying and related issues. Its main website contains links to websites around the world which provide country-specific resources and information on workplace bullying.

RECOMMENDED READING

T. Field (1996)*Bully In Sight: How to Predict, Resist, Challenge and Combat Workplace Bullying* (Success Unlimited) ISBN 0-9529121-0-4.

Tim Field wrote his book after an experience of workplace bullying. His book includes advice on how to record details of each bullying incident you are subject to should you make a formal complaint to your employer and on what to expect from the legal process should you decide to take action as a result of being bullied.

K. Reivich and A. Schatte (2003) *The Resilience Factor: 7 Keys to Finding Your Inner Strength and Overcoming Life's Hurdles* (Broadway Books) ISBN 0-7679119-1-1.

This book, written by psychologists Karen Reivich and Andrew Shatté, is a practical roadmap for navigating unexpected challenges, surprises and setbacks at work and home. Their premise is that your thinking style determines your resilience, and they demonstrate how to boost your mental resilience by changing the way you think about adversity.

Index

A

Abusive interactions, responding
   to   83–85
Aggressive management
   style, as a context for
   bulling   27–31
Assertive responses to
   bullying   70–91

B

Boundaries, bullies disregarding
   your   55–62
Boundaries, managing
   your   70–91
Boundaries, examples of
   preserving your   71–78,
   79–80, 81–82
Bullies, confronting   105–108
Bullies, disposition of   16–17
Bullies, intrapersonal
   motivations of   16–34
Bullies, intentions of 3–4
Bullies, managing team members
   who are   92–112
Bullies, motivations of   16–34
Bullies, psychological profile
   of   16–34
Bullying, causes of   31–32
Bullying, collusive   9–14, 41–46
Bullying, consequences
   of   149–156
Bullying, definition of   2
Bullying, euphemisms for   32–34
Bullying, evolving campaign
   of   127–148

Bullying, excuses for   32–34
Bullying, life after an experience
   of   157–160
Bullying, reactions to
   117–121, 149–156
Bullying, responding
   to   116–117
Bullying, your experiences of
   1–2, 159–160
Bullying, your response
   to   14–15
Bullying behaviour,
   confronting   71–78,
   79–80, 81–82, 92–112
Bullying behaviour, examples
   of   4–14
Bullying bosses, examples
   of   17–22, 22–26, 27–31,
   37–41, 41–46, 55–62, 63–64,
   65–66, 71–78, 79–80, 81–82,
   127–148
Bullying bosses, the power
   of   62–63
Bullying clients, examples
   of   66–68
Bullying colleagues, working
   with   54–55
Bullying dynamic, altering
   the   51–69
Bullying dynamic, creating
   a   52–54
Bullying dynamic, definition of
   the   53
Bullying dynamic, the   51–69,
   70–91

Bullying dynamic, your role in
maintaining a 53–55
Bullying peers, examples of
9–14, 46–50, 85–90
Bullying tactics, examples of
4–6, 9–14, 17–22,
22–26, 27–31, 37–41,
41–46, 46–50, 55–62,
63–64, 65–66, 66–68,
71–78, 79–80, 81–82,
85–90, 127–148

C

Choices, identifying
your 51–69
Choosing not to resist
a bully 84–85
Collusive bullying, examples
of 9–14, 41–46
Confronting a bullying team
member 92–112
Confronting bullying behaviour,
examples of 71–78,
79–80, 81–82, 94–111
Consequences, of bullying for
the target 149–156

D

Depression, risk of 85

E

Emotional reactions to
bullying 151–152
Envy, as a context for
bullying 17–22
Euphemisms for bullying 32–34
Evolving campaign of bullying,
example of 127–148
Excuses for bullying 32–34

F

Fear, as a context for
bullying 17–22

Feeling powerless against
a bully 82–83
First encounters between bullies
and potential targets
35–50
Friends and family members,
role of 113–126

H

Human consequences of
bullying 149–156

I

Interactions between bullies and
targets 35–50
Intrapersonal context for
bullying, examples
of 17–34

J

Jealousy, as a context for
bullying 17–22
Job interviews, selecting targets
at 36–46

M

Managers, feeling threatened
as a context for
bullying 17–22
Managers, turning a blind eye to
bullying 127–148
Managing a workplace
bully 92–112

N

Non-bullying colleagues,
working with 6–9, 54–55
Non-verbal bullying tactics 4–5

P

Passive–aggressive bullying,
examples of 46–50,
127–148

Performance–related bullying
tactics   5–6
Personal boundaries – see
boundaries
Personal choices, clarifying
your   51–69
Personal power, calling on
your   70–91
Personal power, how
bullies want to remove
your   51–69
Personal power, importance
of   52–54
Personal power, preserving
68–69, 78–79
Physical reactions to
bullying   153–154
Protecting yourself from
a bully   70–91
Potential targets for bullying,
selection of   35–50
Power – see personal power
Powerlessness in the face of
bullying   81–82
Psychological profile of
a bully   16–34
Psychological reactions to
bullying   151–152
Practical bullying tactics   5
Professional help, seeking   123,
154

R

Reactions to bullying
114–116, 149–154
Recovering from
bullying   157–160
Reframing an experience of
bullying   83–84

Resisting a bully
70–91
Responding to bullying
behaviour   14–15

S

Scapegoating, as a context for
bullying   22–26
Situational contexts for bullying,
examples of   17–34
Style clashes, as a context for
bullying   27–31
Support, offered by friends and
family   113–126
Support, practical sources
of   123–125
Support, providing
effective   121–125
Supporting yourself, through
an experience of
bullying   154–155

T

Tactics, used by bullies   4–6,
9–14, 17–22, 22–26, 27–31,
37–41, 41–46, 46–50,
55–62, 63–64, 65–66, 66–68,
71–78, 79–80, 81–82, 85–90,
127–148
Targets for bullying, selection
of   35–50

V

Verbal bullying tactics   4

W

Workplace bullies – see bullies
Workplace bullying – see
bullying